How to Survive and
Prosper in a Recession

How to Survive and Prosper in a Recession

A Seven Stage Action Plan That Will Protect Your Job, Your Finances and Your Family

PETER MARTIN

**Hutchinson
Business
Books**

Copyright © Peter Martin

The right of Peter Martin to be identified as author of this
work has been asserted by him in accordance with the Copyright,
Designs and Patents Act 1988

All the information in this book is verified to the best of the
author's and publisher's ability, but they do not accept
responsibility for loss arising from decisions based upon them

First published in Great Britain by
Hutchinson Business Books Limited
An imprint of Random Century Limited
20 Vauxhall Bridge Road, London SW1V 2SA

Random Century Australia (Pty) Limited
20 Alfred Street, Milsons Point, Sydney
New South Wales 2061, Australia

Random Century New Zealand Limited
PO Box 40-086, 32–34 View Road, Glenfield
Auckland 10, New Zealand

Century Hutchinson South Africa (Pty) Limited
PO Box 337, Bergvlei 2012, South Africa

British Library Cataloguing in Publication Data
Martin, Peter, *1948*–
    How to survive and prosper in a recession: your seven-stage
    action plan to secure your job, your finances and your
    family.
    1. Great Britain. Personal finance
    I. Title
    332.02400941

ISBN 0-09-174604-3
ISBN 0-09-174517-9 (pbk)

Typeset in Garamond by Servis Filmsetting Limited

Printed and bound in Great Britain by
Mackays of Chatham PLC, Chatham, Kent

CONTENTS

FOREWORD

Nobody said life was going to be easy; but nobody said anything about recessions, either. Juggling your job, your family, your financial commitments, your hopes for the future, the last thing you need is the uncertainty that difficult economic times create.

This book is written to reduce the uncertainty, to give you the confidence to plan for the bad times as well as the good. It looks at every aspect of your economic life – job, career, household finances, family ambitions, retirement planning.

Use it as a both guide and goad: a guide to help you prepare for a safer, more prosperous future; and a goad to prod you into taking the simple but easy-to-put-off steps that can make all the difference between surviving a recession and succumbing to it.

The thoughts that follow are based on the accumulated wisdom and experience of many friends and colleagues who've offered me advice over the years. I'd like in particular to thank John Kelly, who made the book possible; Charles Target, who passed on something of what they teach you at Harvard Business School; and my *Financial Times* colleagues Peter Norman and John Edwards, who generously offered me their comments. Any errors and prejudices that remain are mine.

The book is dedicated to my parents Jack and Terry Martin, to my wife Sandy Ingram and my daughters Clare and Julia. To all of them I owe far more than I can say.

Peter Martin
London
February 1990

INTRODUCTION

Why the Next Recession Won't Be Like the Last

Every economic downturn is different.

The lessons painfully learnt in the 1974–76 crisis were of little use in the 1981–83 slump. The next recession – whenever it comes – will be different again. For three reasons:

- The shift away from collectivism towards individualism. Mrs Thatcher's message that we must all stand on our own two feet means that businesspeople, investors and families must take much greater individual responsibility for their own survival when the bad times come round again.
- Britain is much more exposed to the world economy than it was even eight years ago. In the next recession, what happens in Britain will be influenced, more than ever before, by what happens elsewhere.
- In 1981–83, the weakest went to the wall. The firms that are left are much tougher competitors. They've learnt the lesson that quick, drastic action can be essential to survival. This time round, expect firms to take defensive action more rapidly, and perhaps more ruthlessly, than before.

Britain will enter the next recession with a higher level of unemployment than at a similar stage in the last economic cycle. It also has a level of inflation that is just as high – in relation to foreign competitors – as at the beginning of the last downturn. If the recession arrives, as some forecasters were predicting in early 1990, in the immediate future, the political timetable will give the Government little time to recover before the election due in 1992 at the latest.

That will probably mean that the Government won't squeeze inflation as hard this time as it did in the early 1980s. As a result:

- Unemployment will rise less sharply this time than in the early 1980s – though that will be little compensation if you're one of the people caught by the rising tide of redundancies.
- Inflation will not drop away as sharply as it did in the last slowdown – which means that the 1970s combination of inflation and economic stagnation (stagflation) will make an unwelcome return.

So for the first time in more than a decade, the recession that some people predict for the early 1990s will combine persistent inflation with rising unemployment – and perhaps with falling house prices as well.

In such a recession, the pain will be much more widely spread than in the Britain of the early 1980s. In that recession, the burden of economic adjustment was borne almost entirely by the minority of people who lost their jobs. Those who stayed in work did not suffer in real terms: their wages rose throughout the difficult years.

In the next recession, however, with fewer redundancies, but more persistent inflation, the burden will be shared out differently. Those who lose their jobs will still suffer most, but there will be fewer of them. Many of those who keep their jobs will suffer a decline in living standards, as their wages fail to rise fast enough to offset inflation. And though house prices may start to rise again in money terms, in real terms they could well stay flat or continue to fall.

The message of this book, therefore, is simple:

In the early 1990s, it is essential to devise a survival strategy that combines protecting your income and career with preserving your family assets.

That's the strategy that the following chapters help you to create – and put into practice.

The economics of the real world

■ When I was studying economics at university in the late 1960s, I was told that part of the necessary education of every student was the subject known by the nineteenth-century name of 'trade cycle theory'. The reason for the archaic name soon became obvious: we were expected to study it in much the same spirit of patronizing amusement as physics students study the phlogiston theory. In both cases, the implicit message was that the theory was a nice try, but had now been superannuated.

The comparison is not quite exact: phlogiston was replaced by a theory of combustion which better described the behaviour of an unchanging natural order. Trade cycle theory, we were told, had been outdated because the natural order had itself been replaced – and improved beyond all recognition in the process.

The definitive work on the trade cycle, we were advised, had been written in the 1940s by Lord Kaldor. It was necessary to study it to pass our examinations, but it would be unnecessary to keep its complexities in mind thereafter, since post-War macroeconomic policy had rendered it redundant. 'Fine tuning', a phrase which then had none of the derisive connotations it has since acquired, had given governments the ability to adjust the level of economic activity smoothly and easily. After emerging from our student days, we apprentices of the economic arts would be as unlikely to stumble across a real recession in our data as to come across a coelacanth on a fishmonger's slab.

Happy, innocent days! This was, after all, 1967, the year of the summer of love in San Francisco. I suppose economics professors were as entitled to the period's illusions of innocence as any of the rest of us.

I may be doing my teachers an injustice here; perhaps this was not what they taught us, but instead, despite their best efforts to the contrary, what we insisted on hearing.

At all events, these comfortable certainties have gone. Since 1970, when I left my studies behind and entered the economics of the real world, the British economy has undergone:

- A reckless dash for growth
- A period of acute industrial unrest and accelerating inflation
- An IMF-sponsored course of austerity
- A further burst of inflation and industrial unrest
- A squeeze on corporate profits so acute as to eviscerate much of traditional manufacturing industry and to throw millions out of work
- A recovery, then . . .
- An accelerating boom, culminating in inflation once again much higher than in neighbouring countries; public-sector industrial disputes; and the looming spectre of another recession

Against such a background – so exotic, so very different from the comfortable world of fine tuning – the relevance of this book is clear. The traditional bankers of the wealthy, brought up on the trade-cycle swings of the late nineteenth century, concentrated their efforts on the preservation of capital. In just the same way, today's ordinary working people have learnt from the events of the last two decades that they must concentrate their efforts first of all on protection and survival. The chapters that follow provide a sketch of how to achieve that aim.

Three economic scenarios for the early 1990s
Since economic forecasting is almost as unfashionable as fine tuning, let's avoid anything so gauche as a single forecast of the

economic prospects for the early 1990s. Instead, let's consider the implications of three different scenarios, all beginning from the unpropitious circumstances of early 1990.

A sharp recession. In 1981, faced with a weak economy and persistent inflation, Sir Geoffrey Howe, the Chancellor of the Exchequer, introduced a draconian budget. The fiscal squeeze, as the climax to a period of high interest rates and a soaring pound, led to a sharp recession. Uncompetitive firms closed down by the barrel-load; hundreds of thousands of jobs were lost. But inflation came down quickly and stayed down; and when recovery began, it seemed firmly based. By late 1989, Britain was in its seventh successive year of growth, and it had created many more new jobs – once unemployment stopped growing in the mid-1980s – than comparable European economies.

A similar scenario is possible in the early 1990s. If the Government were to adopt a policy – high interest rates, a strong pound, a tough budget – which helped to produce a sharp recession, unemployment would rise sharply, from a relatively high starting point. If the recession was deep enough and sharp enough, wage pressure would die away as rapidly as it did in the early 1980s. Inflation would drop too.

In practical terms, the implications would be these:

- The principal threat against which wage-earners and families would have to guard would be unemployment.
- Those who stayed in work would face one or two years of stagnant or only slowly-rising real wages.
- As long as they kept their jobs, they would have little to fear; but the caution and reduced growth prospects of the companies for which they worked would hamper upward mobility.

■ The emphasis of a survival plan, therefore, would be on keeping a job, ensuring promotion despite shrunken opportunities and preparing a contingency plan against the worst.

As far as it is possible to judge in early 1990, this scenario does not look likely. The Government does not appear to have the appetite for a repeat of the sharp squeeze of the early 1980s. Though interest rates are high, and will clearly remain so, the pound is prone to bouts of softness. (Full membership of the European Monetary System, which would help hold the pound firm, is unlikely in the short term.) Tax policy appears to be less draconian than this scenario would require.

None the less, mistakes of policy by the Government or unexpected changes in the international climate, in the mood of consumers or in the attitude of industry could combine to produce this outcome.

A shallow, inflationary recession. This scenario poses the most complex threats. Let us suppose that the economy slides into a brief, not too deep, recession – six or nine months during which the economy shrinks slightly, but not as seriously as in the first scenario. Interest rates stay at their early-1990 level, before dropping once the Government realizes the recession has started. The pound continues to slide gently downward against the currencies of Britain's major trading partners, the other members of the European Community.

The inflation number that makes the headlines, the Retail Prices Index that includes the impact of mortgage interest payments, drops a bit once the effects of the big interest rate rises of 1989 are no longer included in the annual calculation. But the underlying rate of inflation, the one that reflects the price of all the other goods and services we buy, does not drop in the same way, levelling off well above five per cent.

The practical implications of this scenario would be:

- Wage-earners and families would have to guard against two equally worrying threats – inflation and unemployment.
- Those who stayed in work would face one or two years in which the level of their real wages would be dictated by their ability to extract pay-rises that keep up with a constant, worrying level of inflation. Some would win, some would lose.
- The combination of inflation and unemployment would produce an edgy, bad-tempered work climate.
- Because the pound would continue to fall, export-oriented companies and industries would be able to pay their workers better than those in companies confined to the home market. Service industry workers, whose output can rarely be exported, would be harder hit than those in manufacturing.
- A survival plan, therefore, would have two aims: keeping a job, but attempting also to ensure protection against erosion of earnings at work and loss of value of savings at home.

This outcome is more likely than the possibility of a sharp recession. It is the scenario to bear in mind when considering the risks of the next few years. Its importance lies not so much in an estimate of its probability as in the double nature of the threat it poses.

Muddling through. This scenario is essentially a more favourable version of the shallow-recession story. It is also, probably, the Government's favourite outcome. Assume that the same factors are at work as in the previous scenario, but less drastically. Instead of slipping into a true, if shallow, recession, the economy merely slows. The pound drifts downward a bit less hesitantly, perhaps repeating the substantial devaluation of 1989. Underlying inflation does not level off so soon, but continues to rise. None the less, the headline inflation figure is down from its peak of late 1989, so the Government feels able to relax economic policy a bit ahead of the next election. Interest rates fall further and faster than under the shallow-recession scenario. Whoever wins inherits an economy all too familiar from the 1970s: slow growth, stubborn inflation, rising industrial unrest.

The practical implications of this scenario would be:

- The principal threat to wage-earners and families would be inflation.
- As in the second scenario, people's real incomes would be determined by whether they could get pay-rises that kept up with rising prices.
- With a falling pound, exporting companies (mostly in manufacturing) would do better for shareholders and employees than domestically-oriented companies (especially in services). House prices would start to rise again.
- A survival plan would focus on the threat of inflation.

This is the outcome implicit in most economic forecasts for 1990. It is, in the long run, no less gloomy than the other two scenarios; but in the short term it is less threatening.

How big are the threats?

Losing your job, if it involves a worsening of your career prospects, causes lasting damage to your income and wealth. Three months of unemployment can easily exhaust a family's savings, leaving it unprotected against the next blow of misfortune. If you lose your job and cannot easily get back on a satisfactory career track – always a possibility for someone over 40 – the cumulative effect on income can be drastic.

A manager earning £20,000 a year at the age of 40 who is made redundant and cannot find a similar level of seniority in another firm might suffer, perhaps, a 20 per cent reduction in income for the next 25 years. The present value of all those future income flows, adjusted to allow for the fact that, even without inflation, a pound today is worth more than a pound in the hereafter, is £60,000 or so. Taking that sort of future pay cut, even if you do not suffer a day's unemployment in the process, is therefore equivalent to having your house burn down, without insurance.

Prolonged unemployment, with its damaging effects on health and family relationships, is of course much more harmful still.

The impact of inflation, for those people who keep their jobs, can also be very unpleasant. As many people found to their cost in the 1970s, when inflation is accelerating, a single year in which you lose out in the pay-round can leave your discretionary income badly squeezed. You can meet the mortgage, the rates bill, the food bill – but you must sacrifice entertainments, foreign holidays, new clothes.

In every threat, however, there is also an opportunity. People who have protected themselves against the economic worries that lie ahead are often well placed to take advantage of the unexpected chances that all periods of turmoil throw up. Correctly judging the moment to buy and sell – some shares, a house, an antique, a whole company – can be the route to unexpected, but none the less, attractive returns.

The instant diagnosis
To assess how vulnerable you are to the threats that lie ahead – and how poised to grasp at any opportunities – take a moment to do the quiz that follows.

Questionnaire: How vulnerable are you?

Answer the questions without referring to the answers and explanations. Try also to answer each part of the question before looking at the parts that follow. Then turn to the answers and explanations to find the scores. You'll find your rating at the end of this section.

1 What does your company think of you – try to give as honest an answer as you can:
   (a) top 10 per cent?
   (b) 70–90 per cent band?
   (c) 50–70 per cent band?
   (d) 20–50 per cent band?
   (e) bottom 20 per cent?
2 Have you been promoted:
   (a) in the past year?
   (b) in the past six months?
   (c) in the past three months?
3 How did you score in your last performance appraisal compared with the other people in your department:
   (a) top 10 per cent?
   (b) 70–90 per cent band?
   (c) 50–70 per cent band?
   (d) 20–50 per cent band?
   (e) bottom 20 per cent?
4 How did your last merit award, discretionary pay-rise or individual bonus compare with the company average:
   (a) higher?
   (b) about same?
   (c) lower?
5 How profitable is your company compared with the rest of the industry:
   (a) higher?
   (b) about same?
   (c) lower?

6 How indebted is your company compared with the rest of the industry:
   (a) higher?
   (b) about same?
   (c) lower?

7 Is your company any of the following:
   (a) retailing (other than food)?
   (b) home furnishings, construction, or anything to do with house purchase?
   (c) advertising?
   (d) any other industry you know to be cyclically vulnerable?
   (e) the result of a management buy-out?

8 What proportion of your company's sales are overseas:
   (a) most?
   (b) half?
   (c) some?
   (d) almost none?

9 How good is your company with coping with Japanese competition:
   (a) pretty good?
   (b) win some, lose some?
   (c) lose most?
   (d) no Japanese competition in my industry?

10 Have there been any rumours about:
   (a) closing down your subsidiary or department?
   (b) selling it off?
   (c) cutting it back?

11 How high is your local unemployment rate compared with the national average:
   (if you don't know the answer to this, ask your local council or the Department of Employment, which publishes a regular breakdown of unemployment rates in 'travel to work areas')
   (a) higher?

    (b) about same?
    (c) lower?

12 How old are you:
    (a) less than 25?
    (b) 25–40?
    (c) 41–55?
    (d) 55 + ?

13 Have you any professional qualification or experience which would make it easy and cheap to set up as a consultant, freelance or independent operator?

14 Have you any recent experience of moonlighting or freelance work?

15 How many incomes are there in your household:
    (a) none?
    (b) one?
    (c) two?
    (d) more than two?

16 If there are two, and you have children, what proportion of the lower income is left after child care, tax and other payroll deductions:
    (a) 10 per cent or less?
    (b) 11–30 per cent?
    (c) more than 30 per cent?
    (d) we don't have children, or don't pay for child care?

17 Are you retired or about to become so in the next 18 months?

18 If yes, are you on an index-linked pension?
(This is very unlikely, unless you work for central government.)

19 If yes to Q17 and no to Q18, what provision does your company pension fund normally make for raising pension payments to retired employees at times of rapidly rising prices:
    (a) regularly?
    (b) occasionally?

    (c) almost never or never?

20 Whether you're retired or not, is your pension calculated on the basis of your final salary?

21 If you haven't retired yet, calculate what proportion of the maximum pension the scheme provides you'll qualify for when you do. Is the result:
    (a) half to two-thirds?
    (b) a quarter to a half?
    (c) less than a quarter?

22 Do you live within your means?

23 Do you actually put money into the bank or some other savings medium every year?

24 How big are your get-attable financial assets:
    (a) 10 per cent of your salary or less?
    (b) 10–50 per cent of your salary?
    (c) 50–100 per cent of your salary?
    (d) over 100 per cent?

25 When did you buy your house:
    (a) before 1985?
    (b) 1985 to 1987?
    (c) 1988?
    (d) 1989 or later?
    (e) don't own a house or flat, but rent council accommodation?
    (f) none of these?

26 What proportion of your combined salary is your mortgage:
    (a) less than 100 per cent?
    (b) 100–200 per cent?
    (c) 200–300 per cent?
    (d) 300–400 per cent?
    (e) more?

27 If you had to sell your house in a hurry tomorrow, what proportion of the proceeds would be left after you'd paid off the mortgage:

(be realistic: if you live in the south-east, you're unlikely to get more than 80 per cent of the price you'd have got at the peak of the boom in 1988)
  (a) 70 per cent or more?
  (b) 50–70 per cent?
  (c) 20–50 per cent?
  (d) 10–20 per cent?
  (e) less than 10 per cent?
  (f) less than nothing?
28 Do you pay off your credit-card bills every month?
29 If no, how big are your total outstanding balances in relation to your combined monthly income?
  (a) 0–30 per cent?
  (b) 31–50 per cent?
  (c) 51–70 per cent?
  (d) 70–100 per cent?
  (e) more?
30 Do you have any outstanding balances on a store card or any other type of loan which has an APR (officially calculated interest rate) of over 30 per cent?

Answers and explanations

  1 Score 30 points for (a), 20 for (b), 10 for (c). Zero points for (d). Subtract 10 points for (e).
  2 Corporate memories are short, so a recent promotion is always better than an older one. Score 10 points for (a), 20 for (b), 30 for (c). If you haven't been promoted in the past year, score zero.
  3 Score 30 points for (a), 20 for (b), 10 for (c). Zero points for (d). Subtract 10 points for (e).
  4 Score 20 points for (a), zero for (b). Subtract 20 points for (c).
  5 Profitable companies will be better protected against hard times. Score 20 points for (a), zero for (b). Subtract 20 points for (c).

6 High debt lessens a company's ability to survive. Subtract 20 points for (a), zero for (b), 20 for (c).

7 Subtract 20 points for any answer; and double that if you say yes to more than one category.

8 The rest of the world economy seems healthy, and the 1989 devaluation has made British goods more competitive in international markets. Score 30 points for (a), 20 for (b), 10 for (c). Score zero for (d).

9 Score 20 points for (a), 10 for (b), zero for (d). Subtract 10 for (c).

10 Subtract 20 points for any answer; and double if yes to more than one type of rumour.

11 High local unemployment not only makes it harder to get a job if you're made redundant, it also lessens your ability to win pay-rises and may make your employer less keen on hoarding labour through the bad times for fear of being short of staff when demand recovers. Subtract 20 points for (a). Score zero for (b), 20 for (c).

12 The growing shortage of young people makes such workers more attractive to employers than before. Skilled, experienced workers in their late 20s to late 30s are still the most in demand, however. After 40, it's much harder to get a new job. Score 10 for (a), 20 for (b). Subtract 20 for (c) and 30 for (d), the 55 + age range in which employers will often try to encourage people to take early retirement.

13 If yes, score 20 points.

14 If yes, score 20 points.

15 Subtract 30 points for (a). Score zero for (b), 10 for (c), 20 for (d).

16 The more of the second income that's gobbled up by child care, the less financial flexibility it provides. Subtract 10 points for (a). Score zero for (b), 10 for (c), 30 for (d).

17 Retirement is inherently a vulnerable period. Subtract 20 points for yes.

18 An index-linked pension offsets that vulnerability, however. Score 20 for yes.
19 Score 20 for (a), 10 for (b). Subtract 20 for (c).
20 In inflationary times, a final salary pension scheme gives
you some protection against rising prices. Score 10 for yes.
21 Score 10 points for (a), zero for (b). Subtract 20 for (c).
22 Subtract 30 for no.
23 Score 30 for yes
24 Score 10 points for (a), 20 for (b), 30 for (c), 40 for (d). If
you have no financial assets, score zero.
25 Score 10 points for (a) or (e), zero for (b) or (d). Subtract 20
points for (c).
26 Score 30 points for (a), 20 for (b), zero for (c). Subtract 20
for (d), 30 for (e).
27 Score 30 for (a), 20 for (b), 10 for (c), zero for (d). Subtract
10 for (e), 30 for (f).
28 Score 30 for yes.
29 Score zero for (a). Subtract 10 for (b), 20 for (c), 30 for (d),
40 for (e).
30 Subtract 20 for yes – not so much because of the
burden of such interest rates, but because the answer
implies that you've been willing to sacrifice financial
prudence for convenience, something that will increase
your vulnerability.

Now tot up your scores.
If you scored:

Minus 100 or worse
You are very vulnerable to any worsening in the economy (or
to any unexpected blow at home or at work). It is important to
take immediate steps to strengthen your position.

Minus 99 to zero
On this questionnaire, any negative score is worrying; you are
more vulnerable to bad economic news than is desirable.

Anything you can do to increase your financial flexibility and freedom of action will help you reduce that vulnerability.

Zero to 100
Most people probably fall into this category. You're still too vulnerable to bad economic news, however. A few important but not-too-painful changes to your life could greatly increase your ability to withstand an economic downturn or continued inflationary pressure.

100 or over
You're relatively well protected against the possibility of a chilly economic climate. There are still, however, steps you can take to make yourself less vulnerable to recession and inflation. It's worth spending some time considering what else you should be doing in this area.

Once you've completed the questionnaire, you'll have a much better idea of your vulnerability to the economic uncertainties of the early 1990s.
The next step is to draw up a plan to minimize those risks and maximize your ability to seize the opportunities of the moment. That's where this book's message starts.

Seven steps to recession-proof your life
The aim of this book is to provide a systematic, step-by-step framework on which to build your own plan of action. Inevitably, though, some chapters will be more relevant to you than others. As you go through, scribble on the margins next to the passages that touch most directly on the problems and opportunities *you* face. When you've reached the end, I'll encourage you to draw up your own action plan, including only those steps which can most directly address your priorities.
How you assess the priorities depends partly on how you

assess the risks of the three scenarios outlined earlier in this chapter. If you think that, in your particular circumstances, rising prices are a far more serious threat than unemployment, emphasize the anti-inflation aspects of the plan and downplay those that deal with the risks of losing your job. Similarly, if you're most concerned about the risks of redundancy, focus on the sections that describe how to keep a job rather than those that emphasize ways of protecting yourself against inflation.

Outline of the seven-step plan

Step 1 Keep your job and get promoted despite the bad times. The essence of this step of the plan is: the importance of protecting your income by retaining your job; protecting your career aspirations; and ensuring your pay keeps ahead of inflation. This step is valuable to those people who believe in the two recession scenarios – deep and shallow – and to those, perhaps early in their careers, who have promotion hopes which could be hurt by economic uncertainty. The main themes are:
- Surviving the cuts: is your job dispensable?
- How dispensable are *you*?
- Ten ways to make the dispensable job essential
- Adding value to what you do
- Diagnosing your company's priorities in 30 seconds
- If your boss goes under, will you sink too?
- Seven rules for complaining about the boss
- The middle-management trap – and how to avoid it
- Creating a promotion opportunity
- How to get a pay-rise despite a wage freeze

Step 2 Ensuring your company survives, too. The theme of this step of the plan is that holding on to your job may be of little use if the company itself slides into oblivion. It is therefore important to assess the potential risks your company faces, and work out where you can make the most effective contribution to keeping it afloat. The step, like Step 1, is valuable to those who fear recession; it may also be particularly helpful to those with enough seniority in an organization to bear some responsibility for the performance of one of its units. The principal elements are:

- Why you should care, no matter where you are in the firm's hierarchy
- Five questions to ask about your company's health
- Tell-tale signs that the wolf will soon be at the door
- Finding those vital few extra sales
- Cutting costs – three painful steps that actually work
- The instant do-it-yourself corporate strategy kit
- Building for the future while surviving the present
- Saving the bosses despite themselves
- Five ways of getting your ideas across

Step 3 How to recession-proof your career. In this step, at issue is the need you may face, particularly when times are hard, to protect yourself by redirecting your career. This step is valuable to those who fear that recession or inflation may make it hard to achieve the family's financial or other goals in their current career. It may be particularly useful to those at turning points in their professional lives, as they move from one of the Five Ages of Business to another. The main sections are:

- Why the only person who really cares about your career is you
- Is it time to look elsewhere?
- Career planning with a clean sheet of paper
- The Five Ages of Business
- Step by step: the 27-step guide to a new career
- Going solo: who should and who shouldn't consider starting their own business
- How to write an effective CV

Step 4 Salvaging the family finances. This step moves from the world of business to the world of personal finance. It concentrates on the day-to-day financial activities of the household: budgeting and spending, and how to keep one in line with the other, while coping with the unexpected. This step is valuable to those who are concerned about managing their finances in an inflationary climate, or when a squeeze on income may

make prudent housekeeping essential. The key elements are:
- Thinking like a managing director rather than a parent
- The household finances worksheet
- Taking steps now to cope with the worst
- Creating a budget you can stick to
- Reducing the cost of borrowing
- Creating a surplus
- Assessing your investment in human capital
- Building a contingency plan
- Lessening the pain of the big expenses

Step 5 Protecting your assets: investments, savings, home. The second part of personal finance, covered in this step, is the preservation of your household wealth, both property and financial assets. The principal threat to these is inflation, so those particularly concerned about rising prices will find this step central to their priorities. The main points at issue are:
- How much am I worth?
- Five threats to your wealth
- What will happen to house prices?
- Weighing up how the risks affect *your* family
- How to protect yourself
- Taking advantage of the bad times
- Seven ways to turn a crisis into an opportunity

Step 6 Shielding your family. This step addresses the wider issues of protecting wage-earners' families: against loss of income, against the risks of failing to fulfil their potential. It is particularly relevant to those who fear that the economic uncertainties of the 1990s will threaten the well-being of children starting to make their way in the world during the decade. Key points addressed include:
- What do you really want?
- The economic implications of your children's education
- The twenty-first century's seven safest careers
- Protecting your partner
- Making the most of a legacy
- Should you use a windfall to pay off your mortgage?

Step 7 Reducing the retirement risks. Planning for retirement has been made more rewarding, but also more uncertain, by the wide-ranging changes in the pensions system introduced in the past few years. The combined effect of the new rules and the resurgence of inflation could have a surprising impact on many people starting to build up pensions in the next few years. This step will be valuable to those who see inflation as the leading threat to long-term pension planning; and to those whom recession may force into unexpected career and pension changes. The key elements are:
- Two basic, motherhood-and-apple-pie rules
- Nigel Lawson's legacy: the pensions minefield
- How much will I need when I retire?
- How much can I count on already?

Conclusion: How to build your own action plan. This section helps you to choose the steps most relevant to your own concerns and circumstances, and to combine them into a plan tailored to your own priorities. It includes:
- The building blocks of the action plan
- Setting your priorities
- Watching for the economic warning signs
- The first actions to take
- The basic minimum

The price of uncertainty

Perhaps the most damaging aspect of economic uncertainty is the paralysing effect it has on your freedom of action. If worries about the future hang over every aspect of your economic and personal life, it is impossible to live life to the full.

The economic uncertainties of the early 1990s, combining the twin threats of recession and inflation, pose a particular threat to your peace of mind.

Preparing a plan – even one that only exists in your head – is the best way of exorcizing the three-in-the-morning fears that weigh on anyone with financial or family responsibilities.

The steps outlined in this book, based on years of journalistic and business experience, are sensible, practical and achievable actions that anyone can take. As well as providing protection against any bad times in the future, they also offer the prospect of improved performance at work and sounder finances at home, regardless of the economic climate.

It is impossible to peer into the future. But a realistic action plan for survival and prosperity is the best substitute for a crystal ball.

Keep Your Job and Get Promoted Despite the Bad Times

Keeping your job comes first. It may not be the job you want; it may not be the job your talents fit you for; it may be a job you can start – after reading this book – to make plans to leave behind. But for the moment, it's your lifeline. Don't threaten that lifeline: do all you can to strengthen it.

That's even more important, of course, if you like your job or the place you work. The lesson of the last recession is that nobody is safe. You may be doing an outstanding job – but your division or work-unit could still be a victim of rationalization or an industry-wide wave of mergers. You may have worked your way up to a management level that, in earlier times, would have sheltered you against the cold winds – but you could still be affected by the 'de-layering' that wipes out whole tiers of management jobs.

Some sorts of economic catastrophe are beyond any individual's ability to influence. But, even when recession strikes, there are things any working person can do to ensure survival and prosperity. And that's what this chapter is about.

Surviving the cuts: is your job dispensable?
Would an outsider, looking at you and your colleagues, decide that what you do is essential to the survival of the organization? This is obviously an important question: if your work isn't essential, it's time to think hard about safety measures. It's also the hardest question to address calmly and unemotionally. Nobody likes to think that their life is in vain: there's a natural tendency to invest whatever we do with enormous, earth-

shattering importance. But in fact, a surprisingly high proportion of jobs in all large organizations – perhaps 15–20 per cent, perhaps more – are not essential to the company's survival.

That doesn't mean that the people who fill those jobs aren't working hard, or that the work they do isn't valuable, or that a sensible management would immediately axe all of them. It just means they aren't *essential*. When the survival of the company is at stake, those jobs are the ones most at risk. In the pages that follow, you will find a questionnaire that is intended to help you work out how dispensable your job is. Before you start to fill it in, however, bear the following thoughts in mind:

What is the company for? It's very easy, particularly if you have a staff job in a large organization, to lose sight of the end-purpose of the company. Enmeshed in battles with marketing, with accounts, with manufacturing, you can easily forget that the aim is to get a product out the door that people want to pay for. So start this exercise by putting yourself in the customer's shoes for a moment, and ask yourself, bluntly:

How would what the customer buys be harmed if my job didn't exist?

There are lots of essential jobs that do not directly benefit the customer, of course: in the accounts department, for example. Still, this question is a good place to start. If the day-to-day quality, availability and convenience of what the customer buys wouldn't be affected by the abolition of my job, maybe that job isn't as essential as I've always thought.

Look at the big picture. When you're trying to assess your job, don't just ask yourself: 'Could this department get by with one fewer person?' Often it couldn't – everyone is rushed off their feet already.

Ask yourself instead: 'Could the company get by without

my whole *department*?' If it could – perhaps by buying in a service from outside, perhaps by just making do without the things the department provides – then your job may be dispensable even though you and all your colleagues are hectically busy.

Here are some examples of departments that are nice to have, but not *essential:*

- The people who run the executive car fleet.
- The in-house travel department.
- The unit doing analysis of industry competitors.
- The economists.
- The overseas offices that are there because, though they don't bring in much new business, 'we've always had them and pulling out would send the wrong signal to our one big local client'.
- The computer department.
- Half the management accountants.

If your job is on this list, it doesn't mean that the company would gain from axing it; but it does mean that, if the crunch comes, you may be more vulnerable than you think.

Dispensable jobs are often the best ones. But before you rush to transfer from marketing to sales, from administration to production, it's worth doing a little cost-benefit analysis. Often, the jobs that are the least essential are the most enjoyable – and certainly the most sought-after. Examples:

- The research end of R&D.
- The strategy job that involves thinking the unthinkable.
- The part of marketing that's cooking up new product-line extensions rather than finding new ways to sell the same old staples.

These are all jobs that people fight for. They may not be *essential*, but they're fun. And because they frequently require qualities in short supply – a spark of creativity, an original cast of mind – they are often well-paid, too. If that's the sort of job you've got, congratulations. Just be aware of the risk, and keep an eye open for the danger signals.

Questionnaire: How dispensable is your job?

Answer the questions without referring to the answers and explanations. Then turn to them to find the scores and the explanations. You'll find your rating at the bottom of this section.

1 How often do you speak to customers:
   (a) several times a day?
   (b) several times a week?
   (c) several times a month?
   (d) less often than that?
2 Is the word 'planning' in your title or job description?
3 Do you get performance pay tied directly to your own efforts?
4 How many memos do you write a week:
   (a) 0–5?
   (b) 5–10?
   (c) more than 10?
5 Are you the boss?
6 Have your individual efforts added anything to revenues in the past month?
7 Have your individual efforts done anything to cut costs in the past month?
8 What proportion of your time is spent in meetings:
   (a) less than 10 per cent?
   (b) 10–40 per cent?
   (c) 40–70 per cent?
   (d) over 70 per cent?

9 Are there commercial services that do the same as your department?

10 What proportion of your work is the provision of internal information:
   (a) less than 10 per cent?
   (b) 10–40 per cent?
   (c) 40–70 per cent
   (d) over 70 per cent?

11 Roughly calculate the percentage growth in sales over the past five years. Now take away 30 percentage points (to allow for inflation). Is the resulting figure:
   (a) bigger than the rise in head-count in your department over the same period?
   (b) smaller?
   (c) about the same?

12 Have outside suppliers taken you out to lunch in the last month:
   (a) not at all?
   (b) once?
   (c) several times?

Answers and explanations

1 The more often you speak to customers, the less dispensable you are. This rule holds good in whatever level in the hierarchy you hold; successful senior executives stay in touch with customers, too. Score 30 points for answer (a), 20 for (b), 10 for (c), zero for (d).

2 Planners are more dispensable, by definition, than doers. If 'planning' is in your title, subtract 20 points; subtract 10 points if it's in your job description. If 'co-ordinator' or 'co-ordinating' is there as well, subtract another 5 points (unless you work for Unilever, where co-ordination is a higher state of being, and not dispensable at all).

3 If you get performance pay tied directly to your efforts, that's probably a sign that what you do has a measurable

impact on the firm's performance. Your job is less likely to be dispensable (though, of course, if your measured performance is poor, you may be more dispensable in it). Score 20 if the answer is yes, unless the performance appraisal is just based on your boss's opinion of how good a job you've done and not on any actual measure of output, sales, profit or added value. In that case, score zero. Also score zero if the scheme is tied not to your individual performance, but to that of any unit bigger than ten people.

4 If you write no memos, you may be too uncommunicative (or too junior) to be indispensable. If you write lots of memos, you may be dangerously close to that archetype of dispensability, a corporate bureaucrat. Score 10 points for (b), zero for (a); subtract 10 for (c).

5 If you are the boss, of a company, division or work-unit, score 20 (and you'll gain a bit more indispensability when you answer Question 8, below). If you're the boss of the parent company, score an extra 50, making 70 in all. Your job is clearly indispensable, even though you may lose it if your board doesn't like the way you perform it.

6 If you can honestly say that your individual efforts have added a single penny to revenues in the past month, score 30. If the amount you've added is more than your monthly gross earnings, raise the score to 50.

7 If you have really reduced costs in the past month, score 20. (Companies give revenue-raisers higher indispensability than cost-cutters.)

8 If you spent more than 70 per cent of your time in meetings, you may be a bit too dispensable to be safe, unless you answered yes to Question 5 (Are you the boss?). If you answered yes to Question 5, score zero on this question. Otherwise, subtract 20 for (d), 10 for (c). Add 10 for (b), since it shows you're important enough to be consulted. Score zero for (a).

9 If there are commercial services that do the same work as

your department, it would be possible for the company to replace you with outside contract suppliers. Departments that have succumbed to this trend include those providing data-processing, transport, manufacturing and design – and even the post room. Subtract 20 points for a yes answer.

10 If more than 70 per cent of your work consists of providing internal information, subtract 20 points. Subtract 10 for (c), zero for (b). Add 10 for (a).

11 If you answer (a), add 10 points. If you answer (b), subtract 20, since your department has increased by more than the rise in revenues alone would justify. If you answer (c), score zero.

12 Score 10 points for (b), since it implies you're important enough for someone to want to woo. Score zero for (a), but subtract 10 for (c), since at some point your bosses may get round to asking why they're paying you money to eat lunch.

Now tot up your scores.
If you scored:

Minus 50 or more
You're obviously a meeting-bound planner with a co-ordinating role in a department whose work could easily be contracted out. Turn immediately to the pages that give you ten ways of making your job more essential, and start a crash programme to put them into effect. Or think seriously about a different, less vulnerable job. Oh yes, two other things: write fewer memos and turn down lunch invitations.

Between minus 50 and zero
You may not need a crash programme to make your job less dispensable, but you probably need to think carefully about whether your job – or the way you do it – can be redesigned to

give you more contact with the outside world, and a more direct influence on the company's bottom line.

Between zero and 50
Most office workers in most big companies will fall into this band. That's only partly reassuring: the big cuts in white-collar staff in the US have cut deep into this traditional layer of managers and support staff. It's worth exploring ways of adding value to what you do, to push you out of the danger zone.

Over 50
Congratulations. If you've answered the questions honestly, your *job* is clearly indispensable. But *you* may not be, since really indispensable jobs tend to be ones in which your performance is easy to assess. Unless you own the company, don't relax until you have answered the second questionnaire, 'How dispensable are *you*?' (on page 34)

Making the dispensable job essential
If you've decided, after completing the questionnaire, that your job is dispensable and that the benefits it brings aren't worth the risk, then it's time to do something about it. One thing you can do is change jobs, inside your company or outside. A few pages further on, Step 3 – How to Recession-Proof Your Career – tells you how to go about that. But perhaps there aren't any opportunities outside your department, and you like your company, or it's the only local employer for someone of your skills, or you're too committed to the pension scheme to escape.

In that case, you've got to make your job less dispensable. There follows a ten-point checklist of ways to do this. (Alas, those at the bottom of the list are less high-minded than those at the top.)

10 ways to make your job more essential

1. **Get closer to the customers.** Find ways of tying your job more closely to the end-product your company provides. If you're in R&D, can you regularly put aside some time to spend with customers answering their queries and picking their brains? If you're in accounts, can you make the tasks of the production department easier? If you're in marketing research, can you find (informal, under-the-counter) ways of channelling your output to the sales teams in a form they can immediately put to practical use?

2. **Identify new markets.** Every time you get a customer complaint (a formal one, if you're in that sort of department, or an informal one from your friends and relations) think of ways of turning that complaint into an opportunity. A smaller pack? A larger pack? An environmentally-friendly formulation? Same-day service (at a premium price)? Different credit terms in return for guaranteed orders? Specially clear instructions for older people who can't read small type? Try to come up with some sort of quantitative estimate of the scale of the new market you're talking about; then pass the idea on, ideally face to face with a follow-up memo.

3. **Provide valuable data.** No matter what your job, you possess important information to the future of the company – which probably gets no further than the inside of your head. Find ways of turning it into data the whole company can benefit from, by following these steps:
   - What do I know? (Possible answers: lists of most valuable customers; lists of about-to-depart customers; lists of customers whose credit performance could be greatly improved by a systematic approach to debt-chasing; costs of reaching particular customers; costs of doing low-volume variants; rivals' promotional initiatives; top-selling outlets; bottom-selling outlets; outlets that are moving from one category to the other; and so on)
   - Who is this valuable to?
   - How frequently, and in what format, would the recipient like the information?

■ How can I let the top brass know that I'm the originator of this important, profit-oriented information? (Possible answer: a crisp round-robin to all department heads saying you're now providing this information to Sales and would anyone else like it. Chances are, most of the people who sign up will never read it . . . but at least they'll know what you're up to)

4. **Make the data you already provide more relevant.** If you're in an information-providing department, you're probably churning out inter-departmental reports that date back to the Ice Age. Unfreeze them by following these steps:
   ■ Find out what the recipients use them for
   ■ Find out what the recipients would *really* like to know, and how frequently. (They may, for example, want cruder information quicker. Or they may want more accurate information less often)
   ■ Redesign the data-collection and -processing, as far as possible, to get at what the recipients really want to know rather than what's convenient to provide
   ■ Redesign the report itself to be clear, crisp and to the point
   ■ If internal protocol permits, draw attention to the fact that *you're* the one providing all this valuable information by giving it a striking cover sheet or a coloured sticker

5. **Replace an outside supplier.** If you're already providing a service to one department or subsidiary, could you provide the same service to someone else, at no additional cost? If so, perhaps you could replace an outside supplier, saving the company money and making your fate less dependent on the whims of one particular in-house client. (Careful with this approach: it smacks a bit of empire-building. And the boss may all too plausibly suspect that after doing the job for six months you'll come back and demand another three staff because of all the extra pressure.)

6. **Find internal allies.** Most of the other things on this checklist will help you make allies automatically, by helping the company work better. Still, a bit of systematic alliance-forging won't hurt – especially if there are a few old feuds

that need burying. Remember:
- Even if your department is committed to a war to the death with, say, data-processing, you can always build a few private bridges just in case
- Put the greatest effort into forging an alliance with the department that's on the way up (finance or international sales or human resources?)

7. **Find solutions to problems.** Bosses get tired of hearing problems. Getting a reputation, for your department or yourself, as a provider of solutions rather than problems is enough to make you essential all by itself. Curiously, it doesn't seem to matter if the solutions aren't, in the long run, terribly good ones. As long as it doesn't end in disaster, a mediocre solution that's presented on a plate will often win the person proposing it more kudos than a superior solution that takes everybody months of agony to reach.

8. **Latch on to a buzzword.** If the managing director's new slogan is 'Total Quality Management', or 'The Customer Comes First', or even 'Avoid Phone Calls Before 1pm', you can make your job a lot less dispensable by becoming the prophet of the new faith. Put the slogan into practice in your department; proselytize; try and create in everyone's mind the belief that Doing it Right First Time and, say, the payroll department are indissolubly linked. Then just hope that yesterday's article of faith doesn't become today's heresy.

9. **Become a skunkworks.** Skunkworks is one of yesterday's slogans that has a bit more staying power than most. It owes its popularity to the book *In Search of Excellence* by Tom Peters and Robert Waterman. The phrase refers to the curious fact that breakthrough products or solutions often come not from a company's lavishly-equipped research labs, but from a bunch of cantankerous misfits in some other department scrounging equipment and time to devise their innovation, usually in the face of official discouragement. If it works, it's a sure-fire way of making yourself indispensable. But remember, just because you're a cantankerous misfit and your office is a dump, it doesn't necessarily mean you're a genius in a skunkworks.

10. Get closer to the managing director. From the point of view of the company, this isn't as valuable as getting closer to the customer. From the point of view of your job, however . . .

How dispensable are you?

Even if the work you do is essential, *you* may not be. So when the company decides to shrink the head-count, you could be lost in the wash. The important thing here is not how good you are, but how good your bosses think you are. The self-assessment questionnaire that follows will help you try to guess.

Questionnaire: How dispensable are you?

Answer the questions without referring to the answers and explanations. Then turn to them to find the scores and the explanations. You'll find your rating at the bottom of this section.

1 Did your last performance appraisal say:
   (a) outstanding?
   (b) excellent but . . .?
   (c) good, solid?
   (d) anything less?
2 Does your secretary screen all your calls?
3 Has any revenue-raising or cost-cutting suggestion you made actually been implemented:
   (a) in the last month?
   (b) in the last year?
   (c) ever?
4 How often do you make mistakes:
   (a) more than once a day?
   (b) more than once a week?
   (c) several times a month?
   (d) never?

5 Do you pride yourself on your withering memos?

6 If a complaint from a member of the public reaches you, do you:
   (a) follow it up immediately in person?
   (b) pass it on to the relevant department?
   (c) never quite get around to passing it on?
   (d) pass it on with an abusive cover note?

7 Do you have rows with colleagues:
   (a) often?
   (b) occasionally?
   (c) never?

8 How many hours a week do you work (including work you take home):
   (a) less than 40?
   (b) 40–45?
   (c) 45–50?
   (d) over 50?

9 How much time do you spend chatting with colleagues or subordinates:
   (a) less than 30 minutes a day?
   (b) 30 minutes to one hour a day?
   (c) more than one hour a day?

10 Did you get taken to Ascot, Henley or Wimbledon last year by a would-be vendor?

11 How often do you drink at lunch-time:
   (a) most days?
   (b) some days?
   (c) rarely or never?

12 Do you possess any unique skills, unrelated to formal job performance – for example, fixing the fax machine, losing gracefully at golf to the clients or making the boss laugh?

Answers and explanations

1 If your last performance appraisal said an unqualified outstanding, or something like that, tick answer (a) and

score 30 points for indispensability. Score 20 for an appraisal that came closer to (b), 10 for (c), zero for (d).

2 If you're the boss of a fairly big company or unit, score zero for a yes, 10 for a no. If you're not the boss, the question works a bit differently: if you pick up the phone yourself some of the time, score zero. But if you only ever answer the phone when your secretary has gone to lunch, that sounds suspiciously like a corporate recluse – a dangerous thing to be. Subtract 10.

3 If a suggestion of yours has gone into effect within the last month, answer (a), score 20. Score 10 for (b), one that's gone into effect in the past year. Score zero for (c).

4 If you won't ever admit to making mistakes, answer (d), you may be living in a dangerous world of self-delusion: subtract 10. If you make mistakes more than once a day, answer (a), you could be in trouble when times get bad: subtract 20. Score zero for (b), 10 for common sense for (c).

5 If you pride yourself on your withering memos, you've probably infuriated enough people to be an early victim: subtract 20.

6 If you respond immediately in person to a complaint, answer (a), you're a paragon and should be completely indispensable. Alas, few companies think like that, so you score only 20 for your efforts. Passing it on to the relevant department, (b), wins you almost as many points, 15. If you never quite get around to passing it on, (c), score zero. And if, (d), you pass it on with an abusive cover note, subtract 20.

7 If, (a), you often have rows with colleagues, subtract 10. Score zero if you sometimes have rows, answer (b), but subtract 10 also for (c), never having rows: that sounds as if you don't care enough.

8 If, (a), you work less than 40 hours, including work you take home, subtract 10: that isn't enough to make you indispensable in these hard times. Score 10 for (b), 20 for

(c), but zero for over 50. You may be making excessive work for yourself, which won't win you points for indispensability; or you may be genuinely overworked, which implies you don't have enough clout to get assistance. Either way, it doesn't add to your chances of survival.

9 If, (a), you spend less than 30 minutes a day, subtract 10: you probably aren't playing enough of a social role to keep yourself informed and visible, or oiling the wheels of the machine. If you spend much more than that, though, you could be endangering your indispensability. So score zero for (b), the normal amount of chat, and subtract 20 for (c).

10 If the answer's yes, you did get taken to Ascot, Henley or Wimbledon by a would-be vendor, subtract 10. Those jollies are a bit too obvious to add to your survival rating. (Score 10 points, though, if you did go to one of them but took the day as holiday – virtue deserves some reward.) If you went to all three, subtract 30.

11 If, (a), you drink at lunch-time most days, subtract 20. Subtract 10 for (b) – the day you have that extra pint is certain to be the day the boss drops in unexpectedly – and score zero for (c).

12 For the first two special skills, score 10 for each. If you harbour too many, though, you run the risk of blurring exactly what you do in people's minds. So for three skills or more, score zero.

Now tot up your scores.

If you scored:

Minus 50 or worse
Perhaps you take just a bit too much pleasure in drifting back from a long lunch and firing off a few forceful memos. Even in an indispensable job, you may be in trouble when the bad times

hit. Start a crash programme to make yourself indispensable right away.

Between minus 50 and zero
You could definitely do with a bit of image-polishing. Spend a few more hours a week working; try to cut down on mistakes; and make yourself a bit more accessible.

Between zero and 30
Most people fall into this category; but the art of survival is to do better than most people. It's worth making the effort to lift yourself into the next class.

Over 30 points
Good. If your job is indispensable too, you're in a strong position.

Once you've completed the questionnaire – and before you get too depressed – remember the basic equation of corporate life.

Success = Reality – Expectations

Adjusting reality is hard; adjusting your colleagues' expectations rather easier. Skilful management of the expectations of those around you is just as important as skilful management of reality. So don't undersell the difficulty of what you're doing.

None the less, reality is what you have to grapple with most of the time. So let's start by assuming that you're coping with the basics. You arrive and leave the office on time, work reasonably assiduously when you're there, stay sober at work and are polite to your superiors and colleagues. (If you don't do these things, now might be a good time to start.)

▶ If you have serious health or family problems, or difficulties with alcohol or other addictive substances, it is probably in your interests to talk seriously to your boss about them, and ask if the company has any programmes to help. If you think your boss would be unsympathetic, you can probably talk to the personnel department in confidence. In a small company, of course, personnel departments and alcohol-abuse programmes are likely to be unheard-of luxuries. Still, explaining the problem and agreeing on some practical short-term measures is likely to be a better bet than drifting on into a confrontation you will be bound to lose.

The basics apart, however, just how do you make yourself more indispensable? There are really only two rules:

- Make sure that what you are doing is adding as much value as possible – in other words, ensure that everything you do contributes as much as possible to the company's primary aims.
- Make sure that everyone realizes what you are doing.

The next step is to turn those general principles into practice.

Adding value to what you do

Adding value to your efforts starts with a clear-eyed assessment of what the company's aims and objectives are.

What is really rewarded? Attention to:

- Profitability?
- Market share?
- Innovative products?
- Customer service?
- Efficient, low-cost production?

Whatever the company *says* its job objectives are, its real system of priorities is likely to be one, or at most two, of these aims – demonstrated in the way the company promotes people, and in its internal system of code-words and jokes.

Diagnose your company's priorities in 30 seconds

Ask yourself:
- What department do managing directors traditionally come from?
- Are production people a lower form of life?
- Do your colleagues routinely make hostile jokes about customers?
- When was the last new product introduced, and what happened to the person who designed it?
- How rapidly are customer complaint letters handled, and how high up the chain of command do they go?
- Is there a steady flow of anecdotes about how this or that product improvement has been shelved because the financial case for it couldn't be made?

If you decide that, now you see your company's objectives clearly, you really dislike them, it might be wise to start the long-term and serious process of looking for another job. It's hard to do well at a company when you are at variance with the organization's fundamental values. Luckily, superficially similar firms often have quite different value systems, so you needn't feel trapped.

Most people will probably find themselves broadly in agreement with their company's underlying values, however. (The intangible part of the selection process – does So and So's face fit? – is a crude way of ensuring that.) Which leads to the First Law of Indispensability.

Once you've decided what your company's underlying priorities are, make sure everything you do promotes them.

That requires mental toughness. For a start, your boss may have different ideas about priorities; and you may yourself be in two minds much of the time. None the less, if your company's fundamental priority is profitability, you'll gain no points for constantly emphasizing the need for better service for customers – unless you cast your argument in terms of the profit implications of continuing to treat them badly. Similarly, if market share is the underlying imperative, worrying about margins is for wimps.

Adding value in practice. You may have a job in which you have considerable latitude in how you spend your time (or you may be so overwhelmed with work that you can only achieve a small portion of the desirable tasks). In such a case, try to draw up a list of all the ways you could spend your time, and rigorously assign priorities based on the firm's underlying objective.

Then work through the list in order of priority, devoting most time to those tasks which can have the biggest impact in terms of the company's fundamental aim. If, for example, efficient, low-cost production is central to the company's system of values, don't devote a lot of time to worrying about possible product-design changes that might make the product marginally more attractive in some markets.

If you don't have a great deal of discretion about what you do, add value in your comments, particularly written ones. Always cast your arguments for or against a particular course of action in terms of the company's underlying objective: 'From a profitability point of view . . .'; 'With the customer's needs paramount . . .'; 'It is essential, bearing in mind the need for smooth production . . .'. (If your immediate boss is a corporate dissident, you'll need to modify the arguments slightly, to appeal to him or her as well. Don't overdo it, though: assuming you're right about the company's values, your boss's bosses will recognize the force of your argument, even if he or she doesn't.)

Making sure you're noticed. It's an unfair but unavoidable fact of life that people who make it clear that they have serious ambitions are invariably treated better than those who leave advancement to fate. Incompetence plus ambition isn't a steady foundation for a career, of course (though you'd be surprised how often it gets people at least part way up the ladder). But competence plus a polite but firm expression of ambition is invariably rewarded better than competence plus passivity.

Curiously, your peers treat you better as well, as long as you don't get on people's nerves by talking too much about your ambitions, and don't break the unspoken rules of fair play to further them. Colleagues take you seriously if you've clearly got your sights on the top – even if there are no other indications to distinguish you from the rest of the after-work crowd in the wine bar.

Ambition helps to get you promoted; it also helps to keep you safe if the company is slimming down. A manager with a future (even if that future is largely self-ascribed) seems a more important person to hold on to than one who's quietly pedalling along waiting for intrinsic merit to be noted.

So the first way to make sure you're noticed is to make it clear to your boss (and to any other senior people you come into sufficiently close contact with) that you've got ambitions to rise further. If there is a formal career assessment or personnel appraisal system, you can use that (though if it's only annual, you should seek another opportunity at mid-year to press your claims – once a year is too infrequent an interval to remind everyone that they have to take you seriously).

Other ways to make sure you're noticed

- ■ Write clear, crisp memos, with a one-page summary at the front that sums up all the essential issues and makes your recommendation.
- ■ Try to get a reputation as someone to be counted on in a tight corner, even if it means doing things (like emergency photocopying, or arranging late-night sandwiches) that you'd normally think of as below your dignity.

- Display an intelligent interest in the wider purposes of the company; take every opportunity to build links with other departments.
- Dress one level more formally than your current job status requires.
- At those edgy occasions where Someone Very Senior comes to address your department, make sure you ask an intelligent, not-too-aggressive, not-too-soft question. Don't go banging on about an obscure departmental grievance. (At least in public. If it's an *important* obscure departmental grievance, try to catch the VIP for a moment afterwards. But make sure that it's important to the company as a whole, not just to you lot in production engineering, and that you're not caught out trying to stab your colleagues in the back.)

If your boss goes under, will you sink too?

A boss who's on the way out can hurt your career in a number of ways. If you're seen as too close to a boss who falls out of favour, you're marked too. If he or she is too weak or unpopular to defend the department, you could all be victims. And if he or she has no clout with senior management, you may never get the promotion you deserve – simply because the boss can't make recommendations stick.

All these drawbacks are particularly dangerous in a difficult economic climate. In a serious recession, a weak boss may be unable to protect his or her department from heavy cost-cuts. At a time when corporate profits are under pressure, and inflation is high, such a boss may be unable to deliver the pay-rise you need to protect your living standards.

No matter how nice your boss is, make sure he or she is not a liability in a recession.

So how do you tell if your boss is a terminal case? You probably don't need advice on this: the office grapevine will tell you fast enough. There are, however, a few things to watch for.

Signs of a boss who can't help your career

1. **Budgets.** The best indicator of all. If your boss consistently fails to meet his or her budgets, that's a warning in itself. Just as much of a worry, however, is a consistent inability to get an expansionary budget through the annual review cycle. If the senior management don't trust your boss' judgement that he or she can deliver a pay-off on an investment project, they probably don't trust much else about him or her. Everyone suffers some budget-time defeats, of course, and some people habitually submit over-expansionary budgets in order to bargain down to an acceptable level. But if your boss consistently ends up with a steady state, no-change-in-real-terms annual business plan, that's a sign he or she isn't going anywhere – and, unless you do something about it, nor are you.

2. **Memo wars.** If your boss spends much of the time fighting wars by memorandum with other departments, the chances are he or she is going to make enough enemies to do you damage. That's especially true if the people on the other end of those vitriolic comments have a lot of power – the finance department in most companies, for example, or the production people in a manufacturing firm. Some really good bosses encourage their teams to feel superior to the rest of the company; but there's a big difference between *esprit de corps* and a generalized epistolary hosility. This trait is contagious, by the way, so be careful that you don't end up imitating your boss's aggressive memo style. What other people will just about put up with from your boss they may not stand for from you.

3. **Lack of clout.** Can your boss deliver? If he or she has promised to win something from senior management – a new photocopier, a promotion, an extra assistant – and consistently fails to obtain it, that may simply be a sign of hard times. But it may also be a sign that he or she doesn't carry enough weight with the people who count. That may not threaten your career, but it's unlikely to help it much either.

If you decide that your boss is too weak or too mistrusted to help your career, there are a number of things you can do about it. The first, and most obvious, is to get a transfer; the second, to find a sponsor elsewhere who'll ensure your promotion or survival no matter what happens to your boss. But it may not be easy to find a transfer or a 'mentor'. If this is your situation, look back at the list of ten things you can do to make your job more essential: most of them will help to increase your visibility outside your department. The other good tactic is to try to offset your boss's weakness:

■ If he or she has a reputation for failing to meet his or her budget, make sure that your bit of it comes in smack in line with projections – and let senior management know about this (for example, by a memo to all other departments thanking them for helping you to achieve it).

■ If he or she alienates other departments, try to build strong links with them (without ever, of course, displaying overt disloyalty).

■ If he or she can't deliver, try to find ways round the problem with the help of all those other departments you're befriending – for example, sharing a photocopier or a new secretary, or obtaining a transfer for your colleague instead of the blocked promotion.

Whatever you do, don't get yourself a reputation as a grumbling, unhappy number two: the chances are that the two of you will end up posted to the corporate equivalent of Siberia, to torment each other forever. Stay loyal, discreet and uncomplaining, until the moment when you really can't stand it any more.

The best tactic at this point is still to attempt a quiet transfer to another post. If you can't manage that and feel you must speak out, these are the unbreakable rules for a showdown:

Rules for complaining about the boss

1. **Know the risks.** Be aware that no matter how carefully you follow these rules, a full-scale complaint about the boss is *always* a high-risk tactic. There's a better than even chance that you'll end up leaving as a result.

2. **Clear the decks.** Have a polite, calm session with your boss at which you explicitly discuss the central issue you're going to complain about. Thus: 'Joe, I really must talk to you about the commission issue. With respect, I'm not sure you appreciate just how damaging to morale – and ultimately to sales and profits – this new policy is.' You don't have to tell your boss you're going to go over his head; but you *must* discuss the issue that's at the heart of your complaint. (If you don't, you've half lost before you begin. Your boss's boss will certainly ask you if you've raised these points with Joe. If you haven't, at best that will downgrade the importance of your arguments; at worst you will simply be sent back to talk to him.)

3. **Decide what you want.** At the most extreme, this could be to get your boss sacked for incompetence. Be aware that, even if you achieve that, you're very unlikely to achieve the parallel aim of getting yourself promoted to fill the slot. Someone else will be drafted in to do the job, and you'll have a reputation ever afterwards as a colleague too dangerous to handle – or promote. More attainable objectives are: a transfer to another division; the closer involvement of senior management in monitoring your department; the splitting off of your unit, to stand on its own or as part of another department; or a greater degree of independence for you in your day-to-day tasks and the right to approach your boss's boss directly on key issues. Decide which of these outcomes you most want, and which you'd settle for. Decide which ones are unacceptable, too – or you may find yourself pushed into them without thinking about the implications.

4. **Now throw the dice.** Make a direct *oral* – never written – approach to your boss's boss (or to the managing director, if

you're in sufficiently close touch with him or her to do so and if the matter is important enough, to the whole company). Again, be calm. Try not to make your complaint a long, unfocused diatribe against your boss, even though that's exactly what you'll probably feel like doing. Choose a couple of key issues to complain over, and make sure you pick out the ones that affect the company most. These may well not be the points you feel most strongly about – those are likely to be the ones that wound your *amour propre* most, which will impress your superiors less than you. If you need numbers to make your point, make sure you've got them to hand – but preferably in a form that doesn't look as if you've had the IBM mainframe (or worse still, the graphics department) working non-stop for three weeks to build your case.

5. **Expect evasion.** Unless the person you're complaining to has been looking for an excuse to get your boss for ages (which is less likely in real life than in pulp fiction) his or her natural reaction will be to hope it goes away. He or she will suggest you talk it over with your boss, which is why you should have done so already. He or she will try to put further discussion off until after the holidays or the end of the peak sales season or the end of the millenium. This is where it's vital that you know what you're demanding as well as what you're complaining about. Press your preferred outcome as firmly and politely as possible. If things are going your way, the person you're complaining to will ask you to put the proposal on paper.

6. **Pause.** Even if you've got a reorganization scheme for the whole department all worked out on your word-processor at home, allow a day or so to elapse before presenting it – otherwise you'll look too eager. Make sure that this plan doesn't repeat your complaint, or display any rancour against your boss. It should be a calm, dispassionate proposal for, for example, hiving off your unit and making it part of marketing, with a strong emphasis on the practical benefits to the company as a whole.

7. **Be persistent.** Remember, everyone except you is hoping this issue will go away. Don't allow it to affect the quality of

your ordinary work, and don't bring it up every day. But do keep raising it until you're definitely told it will not happen. At which point, unless your superiors offer exceptionally convincing words of reassurance, accept that you've lost not just the battle but the war, and start looking elsewhere.

The middle-management trap . . .

Middle management is the level in an organization at which a career is most vulnerable. Supervising other managers, reporting to more senior executives, almost any middle manager's job fits the definition of dispensability given earlier.

In bad times, a middle manager is costly enough to be a tempting target for economies: not senior enough to be protected from a top-down cost-cutting exercise; but not junior enough to be protected by direct relevance to customer needs and corporate profitability. That is the trap.

It is particularly dangerous now. Traditional middle-management jobs were created and preserved, since the invention of the large company, by the doctrine of 'span of control': the assumption, derived from the army and the railways, that a single manager would be most efficient supervising roughly seven to ten people. Each of these, in turn, would have seven to ten direct subordinates, and so on down the chain. The underlying argument was about information. There was a limit on how much information any one person could gather and process, and much of that information had to be gathered face to face. So the span of control doctrine created both a steep, formal hierarchy based on seven to ten-person groups; and whole tiers of jobs – 'middle management' – which were essentially there to process information.

This bit of history explains why so many middle-management jobs are so unrewarding. Much of the task consists of summarizing issues (with recommendations) that the next tier of managers will decide upon.

In the 1980s, several things happened at once.

The crisis. Many large corporations came under the sort of financial pressure that only a recession brings – the sort that companies hadn't experienced since the 1930s.

The opportunity. Simultaneously, as they cast around for ways to reduce costs, they came upon a technological change. The growth of information technology provided a way to cut out some of the layers of middle managers that until now had seemed an inevitable cost of doing business. Faster, better communications, together with computer systems that provided instant data on every aspect of the comapny's operations, seemed a plausible substitute for many of the information gathering and analysing layers of management.

The outcome. So in many companies, 'de-layering' became the vogue. The 'span of control' changed out of all recognition, as some companies started to load up their managers with 30 or 40 people to report to them, instead of the seven to ten that had been standard before. The new jobs are more rewarding, but also a lot more stressful. So much so, indeed, that in some companies there is now a recognition that de-layering has gone too far. That belief won't long survive the onset of the next recession, however. And in many British companies, slower to adopt information technology than their American counterparts, de-layering has only just begun. The next recession will prove a perfect opportunity to put some of these ideas into practice close to home.

. . . *and how to avoid it*

There are two escapes from the middle-management trap: don't get caught in the first place; and if you are caught, tunnel your way out. Both these approaches revolve round the concept of keeping your job indispensable, as outlined above.

Don't get caught. Whenever you're offered a promotion, ask yourself: How essential is the new job, compared with the old?

(Use the questionnaire on page 26.) The new job may seem to be so tempting – in financial rewards, satisfaction or promotion potential – that it's impossible to resist. But ask yourself if there's an alternative promotion that would offer the same rewards without the risk of making you dispensable. Or think if there's a way of tailoring your new job that will keep you essential – closer to the customer, or to the things the company actually does, rather than to the company's internal information flows. Negotiate any changes of this sort before you take over. It's always much harder to agree even small changes once you've actually accepted the job.

Tunnel out. Once you're in the middle-management trap, here are some ways of escaping from it:

Ways of escaping from the middle-management trap

1. **Move sideways.** Find a job on the same level that scores much higher on the indispensability test. Then get yourself transferred. This may be easier said than done. The alternative is a bit more risky:

2. **Take a step down.** If moving sideways isn't possible, you may have to consider taking a step back into the ranks of those who carry out day-to-day functions, rather than those who plan, co-ordinate or think about them. Make sure, before you do this, that the new job is a good bit more essential than your current one, otherwise you'll be giving up status with nothing to show for it. Assuming you go ahead, the drawback of this approach is that you may have to accept a pay cut (or at least a pay freeze). The benefit, apart from the greater protection offered by a less dispensable job, is that an organization that is de-layering itself may actually be more enjoyable to work in, if power, as well as responsibility, is being pushed down the pyramid.

3. **Make your department a profit centre.** Find ways of turning your department from one that's just a dead-weight

cost to one that makes a profit. Ideally, a real one: if you can find outside customers for your activities, you can go a long way towards proving your department's indispensability. External revenues will lower your net cost to the company below the level of competing alternative suppliers.

4. **Play to middle management's traditional strengths.** The good thing about middle-management jobs is that you know more about what's going on, and you're in closer contact with the ultimate bosses. Make use of this to make yourself important, by building your department – or just your job – into an essential component of the company's strategy. That means identifying what the company's next priorities are going to be, and reshaping your activities to meet them. If you gather that faster turnaround time is going to be the boss's next obsession, make sure that your department takes the lead in cutting its own cycle time – and builds on your knowledge of the company to come up with innovative ways of speeding up everyone else.

5. **Seize responsibility.** Redesign your current job so that it takes in some more essential responsibilities. This may be easier if there's a hiring freeze and somebody leaves; you may be able to grab the more essential bits of the departing executive's job description. Make sure, though, that you don't end up stuck with the inessential bits. And whatever you do, don't trade the essential parts of your own job for somebody else's inessential activities.

Creating a promotion opportunity

When times are hard, you can't rely on seniority or the progress of time to create a promotion opportunity. Job turnover drops: fewer people higher up the totem pole leave to work elsewhere, meaning fewer chances for you to take their jobs. Even if people do leave in the middle of an economic downturn, the chances are that a job freeze will make it hard to turn that opening into a promotion. You may just end up doing their work without a change of title or a rise in pay. Follow this five-stage campaign to create – and cash in on – a promotion opportunity:

Research: spotting potential openings. The key is to identify serious corporate problems or missed opportunities, then present yourself as part of the solution.

Every piece of information you can get – from customers, from senior managers you come into contact with, from suppliers, from junior staff, even from competitors – is helpful here. When you're chatting with colleagues in the pub or the canteen, steer the conversation away from gossip towards practical discussion of the firm's strengths and weaknesses.

Try to build a mental model of the company's sources of competitive advantage and where it is failing to make the most of them (see next chapter). Then think of ways in which, in a slightly different position, with a bit more authority, you'd be able to resolve the problem or capitalize on the opportunity.

Investment: preparing yourself in your own time. Research has gobbled up some of your time already, but the next stage is the real investment of evenings and weekends in your future. Once you've identified the problem you think you can make a contribution towards, you must become an expert on it.

Start by tapping the company's own sources of wisdom: internal procedure manuals, financial analyses, reports. (It's surprising how often today's problem was expensively examined five years ago, by an internal task-force or an external consultant, then quietly forgotten about.) Then move on to outside sources: visit business bookshops and libraries looking for textbooks; identify courses run by business schools and professional organizations that could help.

Depending on your employer's attitude to training, and the relevance of your current job description to the subject you're researching, you may be able to get the firm to pay to send you on these courses. (Even if they won't, and the course is too expensive to afford out of your own pocket, the cause isn't lost. You can find out the guts of what you want to know by looking up the course leader's contribution to the professional literature. You can track down people who have already been on the course, then pick their brains and borrow their notes.)

However, make sure that the issue you're tackling is one that you've got some claims to know about – if necessary, by redefining the problem. Take this example:

► Jane is in sales and has become convinced that clumsy hedging against foreign currency risks is to blame for the company's problems. On the face of it, it's hard to turn that into a promotion. What does a salesperson know about the technical matter of foreign currency hedges? (That's a good question: luckily, Jane's expecting it, and has researched the matter enough to be able to answer it convincingly.)

Still, even if Jane has come out looking surprisingly well informed about hedging for a salesperson, those three words sum up the problem: 'for a salesperson'. Her trick now is to use her new knowledge as a platform from which she can go on to create a promotion opportunity. One possibility: offering to be the sales department's liaison with the finance department, to keep them informed about changing predictions of the timing of revenue flows from customers – and help them improve the accuracy and relevance of their hedging moves.

If Jane's offer is accepted, that's a triumph for research and the first stage of investment. The second stage involves putting what she has learnt up to now to work. This is the delicate part.

You must start doing some of the task you're hoping to be promoted to, but not too much.

Enough to show the benefits, but not enough to put other colleagues' noses out of joint. Enough to display your newly acquired competence, but – above all – not so much that your boss simply smiles benignly and tells you to keep doing it at no increase in salary or status.

Jane's case is on the borderline. It's a good springboard for learning more about the finance department's activities, and preparing herself to sell the idea that there's a promotion opportunity looming; but the extra work involved looks suspiciously like something she could go on doing in addition to her other duties. She'll have to identify extra tasks she can take on – for example, liaison between finance and other departments – and which she can build into her promotion plan. In the meantime, however, she'll have to start generating the oxygen of promotion.

Publicity: letting your bosses know indirectly. All good sales campaigns require both a general, softening-up, series of advertisements or word-of-mouth testimonials, and a specific approach to the target consumer. You're selling yourself, so that's exactly what you should do – but save the direct approach until you've raised your perceived value by skilful use of internal advertising and public relations.

Effective internal advertising revolves around getting the most out of the three staples of corporate life: the memo, the report and the presentation. Public relations involves ensuring that every contactable member of the company thinks highly of you and (more important) speaks highly of you. (For five ideas for internal advertising and PR, see opposite.)

The sale: ensuring that you get the promotion you've created. Ask for it. Then ask for it again. Keep asking until you're told flatly that you definitely won't get it. Don't make overt threats, but find ways of getting your potential foot-looseness across to your bosses (using some of the techniques described on page 57–8). Don't couch your argument in terms of fairness: I thought of this job so you should give it to me. Instead, couch it in terms of effectiveness: I invented this job so I know what needs doing better than anyone else.

Read a good manual on sales technique, and make sure you use some of the 'moving to close' tips that will help you break out of the stalled 'I'd like to give it to you, but . . .' routine.

Consider doing the job without an immediate pay-rise (as long as there's the promise of a review at a specific date within the forseeable future) if it moves you up to another, more important, rung in the ladder. And don't settle, if you can possibly avoid it, for 'grey area' titles, that leave you lingering between grades. You'll soon get over the excitement of calling yourself 'executive assistant to the marketing manager' and start resenting the fact that you're not a proper assistant marketing manager like everybody else.

Five ideas for internal advertising and PR

- *The personalized memo campaign.* You (or your secretary) need a word-processor for this. The trick here is to send influential, carefully chosen people a memo that looks as if it's just for them, with apposite numbers that will help them in their jobs – without looking as if you're running off a round-robin. Add a few personalized sentences at top and bottom (and one in the middle). But keep the rest standard boilerplate. Two Don'ts here: Don't send each person too frequent a flow of memos, or they'll start to feel badgered; and Don't send memos to people if the status gap between the two of you is too great – that would merely look like presumption. Two Do's in this approach: Do try to include a relevant question that will force the person concerned to contact you by phone or letter. That will make the memo look more purposeful than if it's just for information only. And Do hold the memo to two pages, ideally with a clear, concise table in the middle.
- *The stylish report.* It's a fact of corporate life that good-looking reports carry much more conviction than messy ones. So whenever you have something to report, try to do it as stylishly as possible. That needn't mean having the whole report typeset; but it does mean leaving wide margins, getting a proper binder, making sure the charts are done on something better than the computer spread-sheet everyone else uses, and adding numbered pages, coloured divider tabs, an executive summary and a proper contents.

■ *The classy presentation.* Appearances count. Have proper slides made, rehearse in front of an honest friend, dress smartly (get your hair cut!), hold yourself rigorously to 15 minutes and, to get the questioning started, plant a sympathetic follow-up question with an ally. Those skills aside, the trick is finding an opportunity to display how impressive you are to the right people. If necessary, start with those closest to you – your colleagues and immediate bosses – and get them to recommend that you give the same presentation to their peers and immediate bosses. With luck it'll snowball.

■ *Generating effective word of mouth.* Use the Silicon Valley approach: identify the key influence-holders – not the bosses, but the people the bosses listen to. (It's the Silicon Valley approach because that's how you sell computers: as well as impressing the divisional manager, you have to reach the chap with the thick glasses and the ballpoint pens in his top pocket. His official title may be nothing to do with computers, but he's the only one who knows how to get the PC network started when it stops, and the divisional manager isn't going to buy a £1.99 screen-wipe without consulting him.) Also, start passing on nice things people say about your colleagues and they'll start passing on nice things about you. And don't be shy about asking someone who thinks well of you to pass the good word on.

■ *Using the outside to reach the inside.* People are more impressed by comments from outsiders than they are by the evidence of their own eyes or the comments of their peers. If you can impress an influential outsider – a customer, consultant or supplier – enough to get the word back to your own company, you're dealing in a powerful commodity. Also, depending on what your company's rules about dealing with the trade press are, you can use it – with care! – to do a bit of careful image-boosting.

How to get a pay-rise despite a wage freeze

Escaping from a pay freeze requires three tactics that in some ways are the opposite of the techniques just described for creating a promotion opportunity. You'll need to use some combination of the three techniques; each by itself isn't quite strong enough to do the trick.

Three tactics for winning a pay-rise

1. **Reclassifying what you do.** When you're trying to get a promotion, the trick is to find something else you can do to add to your status and responsibilities. When you're trying to beat a pay freeze (or ceiling) the trick is to convince your boss that something you *already* do is more than your current job is worth. Most people do jobs that have a mixture of elements; you have to mentally review all the things you do during the week and choose the one that is most responsible, and most clearly aligned with the company's objectives. (Remember, these are the company's *real* objectives, which may be quite different from the slogan at the head of the staff manual. If you're in any doubt about what your firm's real objectives are, refresh your memory by doing the quiz on page 40.)

   There's one immediate hurdle at which you can fall. If the most responsible part of your job is the one that's at the top of your job description or at the forefront of the boss's mind, the chances are you're already being paid in line with it – so there's little prospect of forcing a regrading that will let you escape from company-wide pay restraints. You'll have to focus on a part of your job that is a little more obscure, so that the revelation that you're writing, for example, a third of the direct-mail copy *as well as* handling the promotion planning will cause your boss to re-evaluate what you do. In all this process, you'll be greatly helped if your boss is on your side. If not, the most effective way of forcing your boss to focus on the desirability of backing your case to the hilt is by adopting the second tactic:

2. **Get a rival offer.** Here again, the technique is the opposite of the one you apply when trying to create a promotion opportunity. When you're gunning for promotion, the impression you seek to give is that you're so totally committed to the company that you're actively seeking fresh burdens,

however onerous, to bear in its service. When you're trying to beat a pay freeze, the impression to give is that your loyalty to the company, which has hitherto prevented you from paying attention to the string of suitors at your door, is being severely strained by the arbitrary imposition of wage restraint. Of course (you add) you recognize the importance of holding down the firm's costs – but the company must also realize that it's in a competitive market-place for resources and talent, and it cannot, in the interests of its long-term survival, allow itself to become uncompetive on this side. Why, only the other day, you were offered this many thousands more to join a competitor. Of course, your first loyalty lies to the firm – but you do feel it hard to expect your family to make sacrifices in this cause. And so on. Points to remember here include:

- If at all possible, get the rival firm to approach *you* , rather than the other way round. (You can help this process along by dropping hints, getting a friend to act as intermediary, and so on.) Not only will this sound much more plausible when negotiating with your boss, it will also make it easier to wriggle out of your talks with the rival firm once you've achieved your pay-rise

- Only use this technique if you're really being offered (or half-offered) a job that's better than the one you're currently holding in most salient ways – title, status, pay, etc. A threat to leave for a worse job is no threat at all

- Since it's usually a mistake to make a direct threat to jump ship unless you get more money (except in firms where hardball negotiating is admired – you'll know if you work in one) you'll need to profess loyalty, but indicate that the loyalty needs to be a two-way operation. This makes it hard to step up the pressure, however, since your boss (whose assessment of your loyalty may well be greater than the ties you actually feel) may think that your all-too-veiled threat to leave is not to be taken seriously. So it's important to bring home to him or her how serious you are without having to be too explicit yourself. The solution is to get a friend or colleague to pass on the message: 'You know, David is really taking this offer seriously . . .'; or 'I hope we don't lose Joan . . . I've never seen her quite so torn before'; and so on

3. **Become an anomaly.** Most pay freezes or ceilings have an explicit clause that allows managers to raise the pay of people who are, by accident or historical coincidence, underpaid by comparison with their peers. (If they don't have such an explicit clause, they very soon acquire one implicitly, under the strain of real world pressures.) So one way of breaking a pay freeze is to get yourself classed as an anomaly, one of a small group of people to whom an injustice has been done that cries out for immediate adjustment. As in regrading yourself, the technique requires you to examine everything you do, and find people doing comparable work who earn more than you. A few guidelines to follow:

■ Anomalies are much less likely to occur in a large company, with elaborate job-grading exercises, than in a small one where everyone's jobs and pay are a bit up in the air. If you *are* an anomaly in a big, structured firm, however (or can make yourself out to be one), you have a much better chance of turning that fact into hard cash. This is not only because big company rules and regulations may actually work in your favour once you've proved yourself ill-treated, it's also because a small company may not even recognize the existence of an anomaly, or may be brutal about it: 'So what?' In such a case, an anomaly is only of use if it can be backed up with a rival offer

■ The more original an anomaly is, the more valuable to you. If you're the only one of the product managers who earns less than £20,000, you're obviously in a stronger position than if there are several of you. Anomaly-finding therefore has little to do with natural justice. For negotiating purposes, indeed, it's best to play down the whole justice issue, because that gets you into areas of ethics and politics with which most managers are acutely uncomfortable. Stick to neutral language: 'Clearly it's undesirable that my value to the firm should be under-rewarded by comparison with everyone else'. (That's why the word 'anomaly' is so useful, incidentally. It's clearly something undesirable, but it doesn't have the tricky overtones of words like 'injustice', 'unfairness', and so on)

■ The uniqueness principle applies particularly strongly where a whole group of people are underpaid. You might think it buttresses your case that, for example, all the sales

managers inherited from the old Toothsome Products Ltd
(now part of Toothsome Morsels Plc) are paid less than
those flashy so-and-so's from the old Mammoth Morsels.
In the real world, it doesn't. The more of you there are with
grievances, the more costly it will be to meet them. So,
wherever possible, try to single yourself out: 'I know that
nothing can be due at the moment about the extent to
which I'm underpaid compared with the old Morsels
people. But that's not the point. The real issue is that the
job I'm doing at the moment is effectively a sales director's
job – and, frankly, I think the company should recognize
that by adjusting my pay accordingly'

All these approaches are vulnerable to the response (spoken
or unspoken) that, 'If I make an exception for you I'll have to
do the same for half the department'. Frankly, only a weak boss
would ever use that argument explicitly; but it's an ever-
present thought for even the steeliest-minded employer. Your
basic view, not necessarily expressed, should be: 'That's your
problem'. If you make your case strongly enough – and if you
believe what you're saying, which is an essential pre-condition
of carrying conviction – it shouldn't be your concern what
other ramifications your action may have. That's up to the
employer.

None the less, the more you emphasize your uniqueness (as a
regrading candidate, the target of outside approaches and an
anomaly), the more ammunition you will give your boss to
resist the fear that giving in to you will open the floodgates.

Conclusions
There are, as the chapter shows, a lot of things you can do to
protect your job, your salary expectations and your promotion
prospects against the onset of recession. Behind them all lie a
few basic thoughts:

- ■ In a recession, it's better to be essential than
  dispensable.

- You need to sell yourself as hard to your current employer as you would do to a new one.
- Aligning your skills and activities with the company's objectives – and making clear to everyone that you're doing that – will go a long way to protect you against the worst impact of a recession.
- Even when there's a hiring freeze and a pay ceiling, you can win yourself special treatment by making yourself special.

Now you're ready to move on from protecting your own position to protecting the firm you work for.

STEP 2

Ensuring Your Company Survives, Too

The chapter you've just read can help you keep your job; this chapter can help ensure there's a job to keep. It explains how you can assess your company's health, find places to make a vital contribution to its survival – and make sure that the bosses listen to what you have to say.

Why you should care, no matter where you are in the hierarchy
In practice, what happens to your company is probably *more* important to you than what happens to your particular job. The last recession – with over a million jobs lost in manufacturing in three years – shows that companies which are often reluctant to fire people individually are capable of firing them *en masse* without much more than a mimeographed statement of regret and the obligatory redundancy money. So, even though your job may on the surface appear to give you little influence on the company's overall well-being, its survival is a matter of pressing concern. It's worth investing a bit of effort in keeping it afloat.

Tell-tale signs that the wolf will soon be at the door
Before you can decide how best to help your company survive, you need to know how serious the situation is. Overall, British industry will enter the next recession in a much healthier state than when it went into the slump of 1981–83. As the tables opposite show, profits are high. International competitiveness is better than it was (helped by the falling exchange rate in 1989).

Corporate profits rise . . .

Table 1 UK gross trade profits, after deducting stock appreciation, of industrial and commercial companies

Year	£m
1984	46,473
1985	55,048
1986	51,011
1987	59,615
1988	68,027
1989	71,705*

Source Central Statistical Office
Note *First nine months at annual rate

. . . but industry's borrowing grows . . .

Table 2 Increase in bank borrowing of industrial and commercial companies

Year	£m
1984	5,719
1985	6,913
1986	8,691
1987	14,950
1988	30,496
1989	42,504*

Source Central Statistical Office
Note *First nine months at annual rate

. . . and bankruptcies start to rise again

Table 3 Corporate insolvencies in England and Wales

Year	Total
1984	13,721
1985	14,898
1986	14,405
1987	11,439
1988	9,427
1989	9,959*

Source Central Statistical Office
Note *First nine months at annual rate

There are some weak spots, however. Industry has moved from being a net creditor (with money in the bank after all its debts are accounted for) to being a net debtor (with debts outstripping assets). At a time of high interest rates, that's not a particularly desirable position. Big increases in real wages have been nibbling away at industry's ability to compete. And import penetration – the share of the UK's domestic market that imports take – is a lot higher than at the start of the last recession.

The picture for industry as a whole may be very different from the position of your own company, however. To get a clear idea of how your firm is doing, you need to combine the eagle-eyed scrutiny of an accountant with the intelligence-gathering skills of an undercover agent. The list that follows should start you off in the right direction.

Five questions to ask about your company's health

1. **What's happening to margins?** Profit margins are the best single indicator of a company's health. The most sensitive calculation is the gross margin, which is what's left from sales revenues after you deduct the immediate costs of meeting the

orders. A company needs a healthy gross margin, frequently as high as 50 per cent, to cover its overheads of administration, advertising, research and development and other costs. Calculate gross margins in past years, good and bad; then compare these with the latest figures. Shrinking margins are a sure sign of pressure on the company.

2. **What's happening to sales?** If sales slow, a company geared up for a faster rate of expansion may find itself in difficulties – even if sales haven't started dropping. Conversely, a company with a (continuing) rapid increase in sales can often grow itself out of trouble.

3. **What's happening to stocks?** If sales slow, stocks can build up very rapidly. Building up stocks gobbles up a company's cash; and if those stocks have to be unloaded quickly, profits may be hurt.

4. **What's happening to cash flow?** From the point of view of short-term pressure on a company, cash flow is often more important than profit. Cash flow (which equals pre-tax profit with depreciation added back in) dictates whether small and medium-sized companies survive. And even bigger firms may find themselves in cash-flow trouble if sales dry up and stocks balloon. Cash flow is the hardest figure to calculate from a company's published accounts: the table that shows Sources and Use of Funds is only a partial help. It's worth asking around among your colleagues inside the company to get a feel for cash flow.

5. **What's happening to the share price?** Unless you're afraid of a predator, a falling share price doesn't directly affect the people who work for a company (though it does make it harder for a firm to issue new shares through a rights issue to raise extra capital). It's important, though – particularly if the company's share price is falling faster than the stock market as a whole – because it indicates the view some well-informed and highly-motivated observers are taking of your company. You don't have to believe them, of course, and the market often goes to extremes of pessimism and optimism. But a falling share price is certainly a straw in the wind.

Once the bad times start, however, you'll need a simpler set of questions, which all boil down to asking: 'Just how bad is it?' That's when you start to watch for the signs that the wolf is really at the door:

- The second set of company-wide redundancies inside six months takes place.
- 'Aggressive cash management' is introduced that's so aggressive your suppliers won't deliver unless they're paid in advance.
- The head-office building is sold.
- A stock or bond issue falls through at the last moment, with no very clear explanation.
- Every set of accounts features a new innovative device, from capitalizing R&D to putting a value on brand names – and too many 'extraordinary items'.
- The finance director leaves in a hurry (score double points if the managing director takes over the finance director's job 'on a temporary basis').
- The board of directors vote themselves a package that provides them with a lot of money if the company gets taken over.
- The share price consistently underperforms all its rivals, and the newspaper City comment columns express surprise that it's doing so well.
- Your Japanese competitors start to build a comprehensive distribution network, and talk about setting up a UK production plant.
- Your company takes on a barrel-load of debt to buy a company in a hostile takeover – and gives 'synergy' as the principal benefit.

Under these circumstances, what you can do is partly dictated by where you stand in the company hierarchy. For the next few sections, I'm going to assume that you're in a position to exercise some independent action – as a supervisor, a middle manager, a boss, a salesman, or a marketing, finance or production specialist. If your actions are a bit more circumscribed, you'll find some thoughts about what you can do to help in the final sections.

Finding those vital few extra sales
This section is relevant even if you're not a salesman. When the economy turns sour, and the business is in trouble, every extra sale is essential – and everybody in the company can help to bring them in. Remember three rules, however:

The 80/20 rule. It's an old rule of thumb that, in most companies, 80 per cent of your sales come from 20 per cent of your customers. The corollary to this is that your current best customers are also often your best prospects for new business. Possible opportunities for extra sales include:

- Selling to another department or another subsidiary.
- Turning what you're already selling into a special package, with extra service and guarantees – and a special price.
- Listening hard to what the big customers are saying about the product, modifying it slightly and charging a premium price.

The good thing about selling to existing customers is that everybody gets a chance to pitch in, from the person who answers the phone to the person who loads the trucks or types out the Red Star sticker. The bad thing is that half the time half the people are doing their best to ensure that the customer not only doesn't add to his order, he or she comes within an ace of cancelling it altogether.

Once customers are established, a routine part of life, it's very easy for people to start treating them as the enemy –

particularly if they think that because they are big customers and loyal ones, they are entitled to special treatment. It's quite common for people – from sales staff to shipping clerks – to be all fired-up about bringing in new customers, and ready to do every last little service for them, while remaining unenthusiastic or downright hostile when it comes to dealing with existing customers. By treating current customers as the best prospects, everyone can help to win – or keep – a few vital sales.

The power of old ideas. Just as it's easy to neglect the potential of existing customers, it's easy to neglect the opportunities for selling more of the company's staple products. When times get hard and promotion money is in short supply, it tends to get hoarded for the new products – particularly if, in a recession, they're slower to achieve break-even than forecast. Of course, a steady flow of new products is essential to a firm's long-term health. But proper care and attention for staple products is vital to the company's short-term survival – and that's what could be at stake in the next recession. Old ideas must have had a lot of inherent strengths if they've survived so long. Maybe refurbishing those selling points – restating them in terms relevant to today's market, for instance, or just reminding potential customers of the product's virtues – will pay off more rapidly and cheaply than putting a gloss on the latest offering.

The power of old ideas is something that everyone in the company can help promote: by restating the product's appeal; redesigning the packaging; reminding customers at order time just how good the product is; or by doing a bit of freelance management accounting to illustrate just how profitable established products are, and how that could be enhanced with a little investment in polishing them up.

Word of mouth: the irresistible force. If you need any convincing about the impact of word of mouth, just think back to the last time you bought something expensive – a car, a fridge, a video-recorder. The chances are excellent that, even if your final choice wasn't the result of a recommendation from a friend, the ones that *didn't* make it to the short list were crossed off because you'd heard bad things about them (or simply because 'everybody knows' such and such a product is unreliable). When advertising budgets are slashed in a recession, word of mouth becomes even more important.

Things you can do to improve your firm's word of mouth

1. **Make a vow always to be positive about what you do and what your firm sells.** Even if you're gloomy, the department's depressed and the company's in a blue funk, try to stress the product's good features, not its weaknesses. This may not seem like much of a contribution to your company's survival, but it's mathematically surprisingly potent. People's networks of acquaintances stretch further than they think – hence the 'three phone call theorem', which states that if you think hard enough, you can find a way to reach anyone in the country in three phone calls.

2. **Write down a list of all the things that happen in your department that could generate bad word of mouth.** Do you arbitrarily transfer complaining callers without trying to find out how you can help them? Do you take more than three days to reply to incoming mail? Do you send people form letters that haven't been revised for years and are guaranteed to infuriate them? Do you or your colleagues do anything to harm the quality of the products the company makes or the service that surrounds it? (Make sure you're feeling in a positive frame of mind before you start this exercise – it can be very demoralizing.) Now think of ways in which you – you personally, not the department as a whole – can start to make things better, starting *tomorrow* . You won't be able to keep up all your good intentions – some particularly irritating callers will still get transferred to the telephonic equivalent of the Sahara, and some particularly troublesome letters will still stay unanswered for longer than they should – but every time you treat a customer or a product in a way that

generates favourable word of mouth, you can be sure you're making your contribution to helping the firm through the recession, carrying your jobs with it.

3. **Turn favourable comments into sales leads.** This is another goody-two-shoes practice that sounds too infuriating to try – until the bad times come and you're grasping for every penny. Again, it requires a little planning. First, find someone in sales you can trust – someone who isn't burnt-out, overloaded or too important to bother with small accounts. (If that means someone inexperienced, all to the good; they won't have heard about the 80/20 rule yet, and this exercise is focused very firmly on those 20 per cent of sales that in good times often seem more trouble than they're worth.) Next, get a pad of paper by your telephone, and mark the top few sheets as in Figure 1, opposite.

Now every time you have a conversation with *anyone* who says a good word about your company or its products, try to see if they're current purchasers, and if there's scope for more sales. Don't worry if the person you're talking to isn't a creditor or a purchasing manager: clerks, personal assistants, secretaries, cloakroom attendants are all influential advisers on the purchase of *some* products. (Of course, if your company sells blast furnaces or mainframe computers, the scope for using this technique is more limited than if you're in the photocopy-paper or industrial-strength cleaner business, but you get the point.)

Most of the form is self-explanatory. 'Interest' means the interest of the person you're speaking to in the product – and his or her interest in recommending, authorizing or purchasing it. 'Past history' means anything you can find out about the contact's past relationship with your company or its products. Don't forget to sign it and put your phone extension on the bottom, then at the end of the day, send off a batch to the salesperson you trust, with a note saying, 'Some of these might be worth following up'. Don't expect the salesperson, no matter how trustworthy or inexperienced, to follow up on all of them, and try to stop yourself asking for progress reports. Just ask him or her to let you know of any successes that come from your efforts – and the chances are there will be enough hits or near-misses to keep you going.

Figure 1

PROSPECTIVE CUSTOMER   DATE

NAME:

ADDRESS

PHONE

INTEREST:

PAST HISTORY:

OTHER:

                        FROM:
                        J. SMITH
                        X 4173

These three ways of raising sales will certainly help. But if recession comes, they may not be enough. That's when you're likely to find yourself caught up – as instigator or victim – in a round of cost reduction.

Cutting costs – three painful steps that actually work
If the recession is long and deep enough, almost everybody in business is likely to be faced with the need to cut costs. Even if

you're not in charge of cost-cutting yourself, you're likely to be involved in some way: asked for advice on possible economies, or expected to put up with the results of someone else's cost-cutting decisions.

It's important, therefore, that you should know what's involved and which cost-cutting measures are likely to work. After all, if you've got to put up with the pain of cost-cuts, you should at least be getting the reassurance that it makes your job more secure.

The three cost-cutting steps that actually work are these:

Get the accounting straight. Before you can start a serious cost-cutting exercise, you need to know two things: how profitable each of the company's activities is when absolutely every piece of overhead, down to the chairman's Jaguar, is spread out over all the activities that support it; and how much profit each activity makes as an operating basis, with overheads stripped away.

These are really two different ways of looking at the same numbers, but the contrast between them is often enough in itself to shock you into action. Many companies don't even break down the profitability of individual activities on *any* basis – often with good reason, because elaborate management accounts are expensive. (Worse, they often direct executives' attention away from the things they should be worrying about – sales and direct costs – to the things they can't do much about: for example, cost allocations as between departments.) 'Snapshot' exercises to give you an idea of the innate profitability of the company's different activities are essential as a prelude to a serious assault on costs, however. Since you're not looking for pinpoint accuracy, they should be quicker and easier to prepare than detailed management accounts.

The aim, remember, is to show them in two ways, as illustrated here (in Figure 2):

BBB PLC Management Accounts November 1990

	Month	YTD	Month v Budget %var	YTD v Budget %var
PRODUCT 1				
Revenues	300	3300	400	4400
Costs				
Direct	150	1650	-25%	-25%
Divisional o'head	59	647	0%	0%
Central o'head	70	767	0%	0%
Product profit	21	235	-70%	-70%
PRODUCT 2				
Revenues	200	2200	11%	11%
Costs				
Direct	80	880	-20%	-20%
Divisional o'head	26	291	0%	0%
Central o'head	31	345	0%	0%
Product profit	62	683	181%	181%
PRODUCT 3				
Revenues	100	1100	0%	0%
Costs				
Direct	50	550	-17%	-17%
Divisional o'head	15	162	0%	0%
Central o'head	17	192	127%	127%
Product profit	18	196	127%	127%
Commodity Division P/L (sum of products)	101	1115	0%	0%
Speciality Divn P/L (from another page)	114	1250	0%	0%
Group P/L (sum of Divn P/Ls)	215	2365	0%	0%

AAA PLC Management Accounts November 1990

	Month	YTD	Month v Budget %var	YTD v Budget %var
COMMODITY DIVISION				
Revenues				
Product 1	300	3300	-25%	-25%
Product 2	200	2200	11%	11%
Product 3	100	1100	0%	0%
Total	600	6600	-12%	-12%
Operating costs	300	3300	-14%	-14%
Divisional overheads	100	1100	0%	0%
Commodity Division Contribution	200	2200	-20%	-20%
SPECIALITY DIVISION				
Revenues				
Product 1	100	1100	25%	25%
Product 2	80	880	33%	33%
Product 3	60	660	50%	50%
Total	240	2640	33%	33%
Operating costs	50	550	25%	25%
Divisional overheads	25	275	0%	0%
Speciality Division Contribution	165	1815	43%	43%
Total div contribns	365	4015	0%	0%
CENTRAL OVERHEADS	150	1650	0%	0%
GROUP PROFIT/LOSS	215	2365	0%	0%

Figure 2

There will be much debate over how to allocate out the central overhead; any basic cost-accounting textbook will give you lots of alternative approaches, and individual departments will latch on to the one that best support their case. If you have a really large figure for central overhead, the best solution is to abolish it altogether by devolving the centrally-provided services to departments – let them buy in their own data-processing, for example, instead of holding it as a central cost.

Faced with slumping sales in a recession, however, that's rather too long-term a project. So try to agree with your colleagues on an allocation basis that best reflects the realities of the business – and use the alternative, operating-profit, set of numbers as a check.

If something shows up as a very profitable activity on an operating basis, but a very unprofitable one (relative to the other divisions) on a full-cost basis, that's a warning bell. Either: (a) there's something inherently wrong with the activity itself (for example, it gobbles up a lot of expensive head-office hand-holding and marketing support); or (b) there's something wrong with the cost-allocation system.

▶ If the people at head office say (a) is true, and the operating people say (b) is true, and the situation's desperate, try cutting the division free. Say, for example: 'All right, you argue that you don't need all this expensive head-office support. So here's what we'll do. You take a couple of the head-office people – the ones you call on most often – or to your staff. We'll reduce your head-office cost allocation to the same levels as every other division – but from now on, you're on your own. If you need extra help, get it in from outside – but make sure, please, that you end up delivering a significantly bigger profit than before'. It's a risky approach, and it can backfire, but if you trust your colleagues to manage properly, it may be the best way out of a hopeless overhead problem – as long as you're prepared to cut back at head office or turn the newly-liberated resources there to immediate account in generating new revenue. If you don't do that, you're simply shifting the overhead problem from one division to the others – and will have to go through the same exercise all over again with the next worst case.

Armed with your new information, you're in a position to move on to the next step.

Setting targets. The aim in setting cost-reduction targets is to combine the short-term practical with the medium-term ambitious. That way you avoid the problem people commonly suffer from when dieting: three months of austerity followed by three weeks of binge that takes you back to where you were before. The combined approach to cost-cutting mingles a deep understanding of some parts of your business with the mindless commitment to achieving a target that is also essential when you are trying to change established behaviour and spending.

Here is how it works.

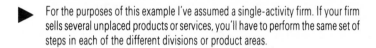

For the purposes of this example I've assumed a single-activity firm. If your firm sells several unplaced products or services, you'll have to perform the same set of steps in each of the different divisions or product areas.

Target for tonight

1. **Identify your three to four biggest cost areas.** These might be production staff, energy, paper, advertising – whatever.

2. **Set a very ambitious medium-term target** for reducing costs in each area. Each has different possibilities, so the targets will be different in each case – but you should be talking big, slogan-like numbers: 'Halve the man-hours that go into this product inside two years'; 'Cut energy use by a third'; 'Reduce inventory costs by three-quarters'.

3. **Set up a multi-disciplinary team,** including junior and middle-level people as well as bosses, to achieve this aim. Ideally, get them to come up with the specific target themselves – but make it clear you won't accept anything less than maximum ambition.

4. **Give the team six weeks** to come up with a fairly detailed plan for achieving the target over a realistic time horizon (more than nine months, less than three years).

5. **Insist they also produce a more detailed plan** for achieving quick, first-stage savings of, say, ten per cent (the same figure you'll be using in a moment for the other cost areas where big medium-term savings aren't required).

6. **Set the target for all other cost areas.** Say ten per cent, a nice round number that everyone understands. Make sure that you're cutting into the continuing cost base, not just making one-off savings.

7. **Don't let people cheat.** The commonest dodges: shifting costs on to another department; comparing apples with oranges (for example, this year's costs with last year's); offering up 'paper' cuts (for example, unfilled positions they never intended to use). And remember: small things add up.

8. **Make sure there's a deadline.** For example, the beginning of the next quarter. And stick to it: get all the cost-cuts promised *and implemented* by the deadline, then give people a breathing space. You'll still be getting the medium-term effect of your more ambitious cost-cutting plans, and you can always do the whole exercise all over again in a year's time – but in the meantime, people need the reward of having accomplished a painful duty and putting it behind them.

Trim lines of business, too. The first two steps assume you keep all your revenue-generating activities, but hope to perform them more cheaply. Really big cost savings, however, can often only be achieved by tackling the question of whether you should be in some businesses (or parts of your product range) at all. During the good years, companies usually allow their core businesses to be encrusted with a layer of additional products and services. That makes sense – some of them may grow up to be big money-makers themselves, and in any case, they serve as a useful competitive weapon, crowding out potential rivals.

In a recession, though, some of these marginal activities are doubly draining. Not only do they tie up capital that could be better used to repay debt or expand the healthier parts of the business, they also tie up the time of managers who could earn better returns on their efforts in other parts of the business.

In assessing the value of a firm's activities, the two accounting calculations you did right at the start come into play.

Judging the businesses

1. **Start by looking at the profitability calculations** that spread out the firm's overheads across all its lines of business. As a general rule, some of these activities will be markedly less profitable than others – or they may be lossmakers. (If the unsatisfactory lines of business are important in revenue terms – they may even be the firm's core activity – then you cannot easily consider lopping them off: your efforts will have to be focused on salvaging them by other means. If alongside such an ailing core business, there is a smaller, slightly less unprofitable sideline, consider closing that down to devote all your attention to the sick core.)

2. **Once you've identified the least profitable activities,** try to calculate what the impact on the firm of closing them down would be. The operating profit calculations give you a starting point. The difference between each activity's profit on an operating basis and its profit (or loss) on a fully-loaded basis is the contribution the activity makes to corporate overhead. If you close the activity down, you'll have to cope with this portion of overhead somehow, either by eliminating it (making head-office managers redundant, sorting out office space, etc) or by spreading it out over the firm's other activities.

3. **Now be careful.** If the activity under scrutiny makes a substantial contribution to corporate overhead, and its removal cannot be offset by eliminating head-office costs, then spreading out the overhead will merely make the firm's other activities look less profitable. That can start you on a downward spiral of revenues and profits in which you forever cut off activities which contribute to corporate overhead, without making the cuts in those overheads that would bring the business back into balance.

4. A perfect candidate for elimination will often be revealed by this analysis, however: an activity that makes a fairly large loss, but which – because of its small revenues – makes a relatively small contribution to corporate overhead. Closing that activity down – especially if you can make some head-office savings at the same time – will eliminate a source of losses and free the time of senior executives which would otherwise be spent worrying about it.

Cutting costs is never pleasant. But it's very easy for a company to allow itself to drift, during the good years, into a state of mindless and blocked diversification. In a recession, persisting in such attitudes can damage even the healthy parts of the firm.

The instant do-it-yourself corporate strategy kit

Unless you're running a business unit, cost-cutting is something more likely to have been done to you than something you do yourself. On the face of it that might seem to apply to strategic planning, too. In fact, though, anyone can – and should – do their own corporate strategizing, if only to work out which parts of the firm hold the most promise (in order to arrange a transfer there) or whether the firm has a future at all (in order to take the steps outlined in the next chapter).

Corporate strategy, as taught in business schools and practised in large corporations, is an enormously labour-intensive and long-winded activity, filled with grindingly dull market analysis and lots of flashy diagrams.

In fact, though, you can do enough strategizing to help you plan your own future fairly quickly. And a lot of the best and most strategically-run companies get that way by the quality of the thought employees at all levels put into their daily activities, not by separating out that intelligent thinking and calling it a separate name.

To start your own instant do-it-yourself corporate strategy, turn to the step-by-step procedures that follow. But first, remember the basic economic underpinnings of corporate life.

In A-level economics, they teach you that in a truly competitive market, all the participants earn what are called 'normal profits'. Everything else ('supernormal profits') is competed away. That sounds fine, especially if you're an academic economist and not a businessperson, until you consider what 'normal profits' actually are. Answer: the rate of return on a riskless investment, plus a risk premium for the activity you're undertaking. (The risk premium isn't a bonus, no matter how big it is – it's the equivalent of an insurance policy which offsets the fact that, in a risky business, something will inevitably go wrong sometime.)

The plain fact is that normal profits aren't really enough by contemporary stock-market standards. They may be good enough for economists, but they aren't likely to be very attractive to your boss, or to a performance-driven investment manager. What the markets are looking for is companies that regularly earn *supernormal* profits.

There are really only two ways to earn supernormal profits: having lower costs than your competitors; or being able to extract a higher price than rival firms.

Lower costs are obvious; extracting a higher price is only really achieved by exploiting an element of market dominance. That market dominance is a form of monopoly power.

In its crudest form, it can indeed be a true monopoly: cellular radio in Britain is very profitable because there are only two networks; commercial television has traditionally been a 'licence to print money' because in each region of Britain only one television station has been allowed to sell television advertising. At a more mundane level, yours may be the only chip shop opposite the town's busiest pub.

The monopoly may be more subtle, however: you may have sole rights to your own brand name and people have spent many years learning to trust that – which gives you a bit of monopoly power and licence to raise your prices a little (not too much, though – brand names only give you an element of market dominance). Or you may possess a unique production technique which allows you, for example, to exploit a particularly convenient form of packaging. And so on.

The essence of running a satisfactorily profitable company, therefore, is to possess a cost or price advantage in at least one line of business. And the essence of corporate strategy is to build the company's future around such advantages.

This simple truth lies behind all the diagrams, matrices and competitive analyses normally trotted out in the cause of corporate strategy. Once you grasp it, you need never puzzle out a diagram again. Since you will need to impress your colleagues with your strategic vision, however, you might find it helpful to master the diagram opposite (Figure 3), and to think through where your company's lines of business and services actually are.

Use the chart to plot the position of your main product lines on two axes: 'costs', relative to your competitors; and 'monopoly power', for example, brand strength, market share, distribution, and so on.

There are basically five zones you can end up in. I've called them Commodity Corner, Black Hole, the Primrose Path, Profitless Prosperity and Nirvana. To take them in turn:

- COMMODITY CORNER is a zone in the south-west corner, with low monopoly power and low costs. It is often an unpleasant place to be, since profits depend entirely on keeping your costs below your rivals, something that's particularly difficult with free trade and volatile exchange rates.
- BLACK HOLE is the nastiest zone, in the south-east corner, with high costs and low pricing power. A business in the Black Hole is in big trouble, and urgent action is required: disposal,

Figure 3

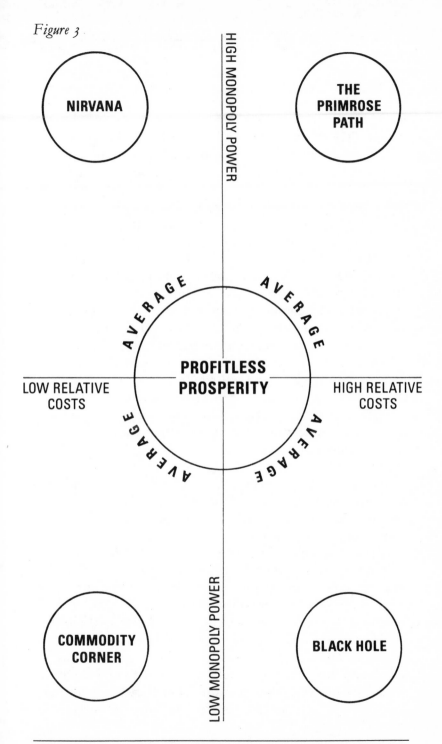

NIRVANA

THE PRIMROSE PATH

HIGH MONOPOLY POWER

AVERAGE AVERAGE

LOW RELATIVE COSTS

PROFITLESS PROSPERITY

HIGH RELATIVE COSTS

AVERAGE AVERAGE

COMMODITY CORNER

BLACK HOLE

LOW MONOPOLY POWER

drastic cost-cuts, crash R&D programme (to create monopoly power), etc.

- THE PRIMROSE PATH is superficially attractive, in the north-east corner, where high monopoly power allows you to do well despite high costs. It leads to damnation at some point, however, if you allow your monopoly power to erode. Until then, it's very pleasant for shareholders, managers and workers alike.
- PROFITLESS PROSPERITY lies in the middle, where the axes cross. Average costs and average monopoly power give you little opportunity to achieve supernormal returns. It's fine for some (perhaps most) of your businesses – as long as you also have revenues from more favoured quarters.
- NIRVANA in the north-west quadrant is just what its name implies, where low relative costs and high monopoly power combine to produce supernormal profits. Make sure you stay there! And make sure your prices reflect your market position, not your costs.

In most cases, corporate strategy boils down to the attempt to move your firm's centre of gravity towards the north-west, and to hold it there. Thinking strategically is therefore the simple act of asking yourself before you take any decision of substance: Which direction does this decision move us in? If it's not towards the north-west, why am I taking it? Note that this approach is not just for chief executives: it applies to every level of decision making in the company. Will this brochure increase my 'monopoly power', by contributing to the aura of the brand? Will shifting to the new package result in a cost advantage against my rivals?

Usually, of course, you will be faced with a trade-off. A decision will move you south-west or north-east, and you have to assess whether the drop in costs justifies the sacrifice of market position, or the strengthening of the brand justifies the higher costs involved. The one thing you should always beware of, however, is a decision that moves you south-east, towards the Black Hole. Surprisingly, companies repeatedly make such decisions, usually in the illusory search for volume.

That's the background. Here's how to put it into practice. For everything except the very last step (How Does it All Add Up?), work at the level of your component business.

The sequence that follows is a step-by-step guide to drawing up a strategic analysis, even one that only exists in your head. It's illustrated with the sort of slides you would want to put together if you intended to use the analysis for briefing your colleagues.

Where you stand now

1. **What business are you in?** In some ways this is the trickiest question of them all.

First, are you in the glue business, or the business of solving adhesion problems? That is, how widely should you draw the boundaries of what you do? Set the boundaries too wide, and you lose your ability to derive useful conclusions from your study (and almost certainly underestimate your ability to extract premium pricing, since you will exaggerate the number of competitors and shrink your market share calculations).

Draw the boundaries too narrow, and you close off fruitful strategic moves, limit your ability to exploit your brand names and fail to spot potential competitors.

AMALGAMATED SLUDGE
- Sludge removal
- Sale of sludge products

SLUDGE REMOVAL
- Taking away and disposing of industrial sludge

SLUDGE SALE
- Industrial sales
- Retail sales – bulk
- Retail sales – premium

(If you're in the carbon-paper business, your rivals are other carbon-paper makers. If you're in the business of facilitating copy-making, your rivals include that funny little company from Rochester, New York State. What's it called? Oh yes, Xerox.)

Second, are your products in the same business? Or are the market segments to which they sell so different as to constitute different businesses with different competitors and demand factors in each?

2. Who are your competitors? If you've defined the business correctly, the competitors are obvious. How much do you really know about them, however? Pick up the phone and call a couple of customers who are familiar with the competitors. Pull together some market-share numbers. Buy one of those inter-company comparison studies. Write down on a piece of paper what the competitors offer at each price point. See if anyone in the company (or among its outside contacts) knows the competition's costs. You can spend forever on this task alone, so don't overdo it; but do try to think systematically about your competition.

PREMIUM SALES
Competition
- Universal Sludge 17%
- Sludge GmbH 22%
- Seiko sludge 11%

UNIVERSAL SLUDGE
- Very strong in north
- Outdated plant, high costs
- Good distribution, no discounts

> **PREMIUM SALES**
> ■ No. 2 in market
> ■ Price leader
> ■ Margins ok, but under pressure
> ■ Real sales growth 4% per annum

3. **How are you doing?** What's your market share? Is it rising or falling? Are you strong in premium products or in commodity areas? Are you one of the top two competitors or down among the also-rans? Have you any pricing flexibility? What's been happening to volumes? Sales in inflation-adjusted money? Variable costs? Gross margins? Overheads? Net margins?

Again, you can spend as little or as long on this expense as you like. Make sure you know the broad-brush answer to each of these questions, however, before moving on.

Where you'll be in five years

> **PREMIUM SLUDGE**
> ■ Long-term growth 7% per annum
> ■ Market fragmenting
> ■ Strong export prospects

4. **What are the growth prospects?** A simple question. Is the market growing, shrinking or stable? Is it fragmenting or coalescing? Try to put a number on the amount you expect demand to grow in real terms.

> **KEY FACTORS**
> ■ Gardening demand
> ■ Processing technology
> ■ Distribution channels
> ■ Branding

5. **What forces drive the business?** Technology? Demographics? Changing tastes? Disposable income? New entrants? Globalization? 1992? Commoditization? Differentiation? And so on.

NO-CHANGE SCENARIO
■ Still no. 2, market share static
■ Margins under pressure
■ Growing Japanese threat

6. **Where will you be in five years?** If you don't take drastic action, that is. Where will the pressures outlined in the questions up to now push you. To market leadership? Back among the also-rans? Towards extinction?

Doing something about it

FIVE-YEAR TARGET
■ No. 1, more than 30% market share
■ Margins stabilized
■ 40% of sales overseas

7. **Where do you want to be in five years?** if you do take drastic action. Now that you've got some idea of what's realistic, sketch out some goals. Market leadership? Out of the pack? Out of the business altogether?

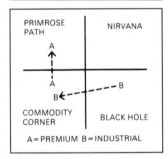

8. **Which way should you move the business – and how?** Remember the strategy diagram.

   Ideally, of course, you'd like to be in Nirvana, the north-west quadrant. But if you can't get there:

■ How do you get out of the Black Hole?
■ If you're in Commodity Corner, the south-west quadrant, and likely to stay there, how can you focus all your efforts on moving further west, towards long-term cost advantage?

STRATEGIC MOVES
- Premium: higher market power, lower costs
- Industrial: less branding, big cost cut

- If you're on the Primrose Path, in the north-east quadrant, how can you ensure that your market dominance stays high? Can you prevent your high costs from spiralling out of control? Are there competitors about to make big strides on cost?

- If you're trapped in Profitless Prosperity, round the centre of the diagram, how are you going to stop yourself sliding towards the south-east?

- If you've attained Nirvana, in the north-west quadrant, can you be sure you'll stay there?

PROFIT AS % SALES

	Now	5 Years
Removal Sales	8	8
–Industrial	12	11
–Retail, bulk	12	10
–Premium	5	16

PROFIT

	Now	5 Years
Removal Sales	100	120
–Industrial	40	45
–Retail, bulk	30	70
–Premium	5	120

9. **How does it all add up?** Now that you've carried out this exercise for each component business, add it all together and allow for corporate overhead. Does the plan still look realistic? Are you sacrificing so much volume in your rush north-east that you're losing the ability to absorb overhead? Will the sacrifices planned for businesses A and B (in the interests of long-term health) be offset by the short-term profit-taking in businesses C and D? Will the total margin be satisfactory in five years' time? Would you buy a share in this company?

Pulling it all together

PRINCIPLES
- General strategy for retail
- High added value strategy for premium
- Lowest cost producer essential for industrial, retail markets

ACTION
- Task force on cost cuts
- Relaunch brand in premium market
- Cancel planned retail, bulk advertising campaign
- Strengthen northern distribution

10. **What practical steps must you take now?** What broad principles must you adopt to guide your actions in the next few years? What must you definitely avoid?

Building for the future while surviving the present

The corporate strategy exercise is mostly about the future: your pay cheque is mostly about the present. Linking the two isn't easy. As the title of this section suggests, the process is a double one: you must not sacrifice the prospects of a healthy company in five years time, but you must also ensure that the company survives to inherit that healthy future. Here are some questions to ask, therefore, whenever you are asked to approve (or go along with) some action because of its future benefit.

- When is the pay-off? How big is it? How specific are the projections? Who'll be accountable if they aren't met? (If it's someone else's project, but you'll end up carrying the can, that's a pretty good reason for scepticism all by itself.)
- If the market shrinks by five per cent in the next year, how will this project look? Similarly, if it shrinks by 20 per cent?
- If the project is to improve our image or strengthen our position, just exactly how will that translate into higher prices (after inflation) than we'd otherwise have been able to change?
- If it's a promotion or advertising project, how do we intend to measure its impact?
- If it's an extra staff position, where will the extra revenues come from to ensure that our revenue/staff ratio doesn't fall?
- If it's a new machine, are we really sure that the person proposing it isn't driven as much by techno-lust as by economics? (Be especially careful of a request for computers and printing machinery. For some reason, in-house print managers and data-processing departments share a belief that companies only exist to buy them new toys.)
- If it's to give us extra information (for marketing or finance, for example) do we really need the data? (This is a very heretical question.)

And some questions to ask whenever you're invited to do something because of its urgent and immediate necessity for survival:

- Is this hurting or helping the parts of the company that provide goods and services to the customer?

If hurting, can't we direct the hurt to a bit of the firm that's less essential?
- If I were a Japanese manager, would I do this?
- Can I be more radical?
- How will this decision look next year when every percentage point of market share is vital?

Saving the bosses despite themselves

Much of this chapter will only have been of theoretical interest to people who don't run a business unit. The way to make it practically relevant to your own prospects in a recession is to get the insights you've gathered from this chapter across to your bosses.

Five ways of getting your ideas across

1. **Sound out the powers that be.** Find out, directly or indirectly, which factions of senior management are receptive to your nearly crystallized ideas. If none of them are, you'll have to be extra cautious. If some of them are, you've got a ready made audience – but be careful that your strategizing doesn't end up as ammunition in someone's power game. And check that your own boss isn't implacably opposed to your ideas; his or her hostility won't rule out a bit of gentle proselytizing, but it'll have to be more discreet and tentative.

2. **Make the general specific.** Don't put your view in terms of a general theory, put it in terms of the discrete actions and consequences that flow from it. Thus, don't say, 'I'm trying to move into the north-east quadrant on a cost/market dominance axis', say, 'Some quick and dirty market research suggests we can add two points to our gross margin by redesigning the pack to stress the product's unique sludge action'.

3. **Put analysis into routine reports.** You may not have easy access to senior managers, and the corporate culture probably discourages firing off cosmic memos to the people on the top floor. But you almost certainly produce some documents that

are read higher up – routine reports, budget submissions, etc.
Start adding a paragraph (or a page) of analysis, as concrete
as possible. And if you don't produce a routine report,
consider doing so, to act as a conduit or for your ideas.

4. **Build alliances.** Not just with bosses, but with colleagues at
   your level in different departments. Not only will you be able
   to get more weight behind your message, it will also be better
   for exposure to departmental views and knowledge you
   haven't considered before. Just be careful not be seen as
   'plotting'.

5. **Don't push your luck.** If you do start to become influential,
   don't infuriate everyone (especially your boss) by boasting
   about your contacts with the high and mighty. 'As I was
   saying to the MD the other day . . .' is a sure-fire way of
   making sure that even if the boss hangs on every word you
   say, your co-workers will automatically tune it out.

Conclusion

Surviving the recession is in part a collective effort. No matter
how good you are at your job, you can run into trouble if your
firm does. Helping your company cope with the next recession
is in part a matter of keeping an eye out for the danger signs; in
part a matter of coping with short-term cost and sales
problems; and in part a question of thinking through the
company's future strategy. Doing all these things will add
immeasurably to your chances of coming out of the recession
in better shape than you – and your company – went in.

How to Recession-Proof Your Career

Even if you keep your job and preserve your standard of living, a recession can still cause lasting damage to your career:

- By weakening your company, a recession can leave it vulnerable to takeover, pushing you further down the corporate pecking order.
- By making it harder to achieve your budgeted goals, a recession can damage your performance record, harming your prospects for further promotion.
- And by forcing your firm to retrench, a recession can close off expansion possibilities that would have supplied a fruitful flow of new promotion opportunities in the future.

Obviously, a recession is a bad time to change jobs, as the shrinking appointments vacant sections of the newspapers will show all too clearly. But it is not necessarily a bad time to plan a complete change of career: even if the recession itself prevents you from putting those plans into operation immediately, they would be ready and waiting when the outlook improves and the prospects of moving look rosier.

And planning is the important word here; remember the first of two harsh truths of business life:

The only person who really cares about your career is you.

The first law is particularly hard to grasp if you work in a large company with a human resource department, career development discussions and all the paraphernalia of new wave personnel policies. 'People are our most important resource,' your bosses say; and they may even mean it. But you're not *people*, you're you. What's good for you as an individual may be something quite different from what's good for 'people' or for the company as a whole.

The main threat, though, comes not so much from a corporate personnel master plan that doesn't suit your needs, but from an exaggerated belief that 'someone up there is watching over my career'. Alas, in all but a handful of companies, career development proceeds by accident rather than system and you must actively seek out opportunities yourself.

When you realize, usually in your 30s, that there is no company blueprint that will take you smoothly to main-board director, it's easy – and dangerous – to over-react. At this point, you risk falling foul of the second harsh law of career development:

Serendipity is a very poor basis for career planning.

When you're depressed by a setback at work, it's tempting to respond to the next good opportunity that comes along – an ad in the paper that fits your experience exactly, a phone call from a headhunter, a chance meeting with an old friend who just happens to be looking for a finance director. The opportunity may be a good one. But if you haven't thought through what you want from your next job, you may find yourself trapped by the same factors that are causing you trouble in your current job and thus no happier or better off.

That's why the first three sections of this chapter tell you how to assess what's right for the next step in your career. Even if you're perfectly happy with what you're doing now, it's worth working your way through the questions: they'll help you to get the message of what you want across to your boss, and guide you when the next unexpected opportunity opens up.

How to tell when it's time to look elsewhere

People who achieve any success in life are usually experts at deferred gratification: don't go out with the lads, wait until after your GCSEs; don't leave school early, stay for your A-levels; don't take that well-paid school-leaver's job, go to university; and so on.

The trouble is that deferred gratification becomes a habit, and you never stop to notice that what you're deferring is your life. The essence of career planning is to face up explicitly to the trade-offs you're making and the objectives you hope to achieve. You need to ask a number of basic questions:

How happy are you with your job? Under this heading are issues such as: how much does the job make use of your skills; how satisfied are you with the pay and perks; what sort of promotion possibilities are there; what sort of messages are you getting from your bosses about your future; are you getting enough useful experience (for example, of international business); and so on.

How happy are you with your company? Is it the sort of company you're proud to work for? Is it big enough to suit your ambitions/not small enough to suit your preference for entrepreneurialism? Is it making a satisfactory return for shareholders? How vulnerable is it to a takeover? How well placed is it for the intensifying international competition of the next decade?

How happy are you with your life? Do you generally feel optimistic and enthusiastic at the prospect of returning to work after a holiday? Do you spend enough time with your family? Is your commuting pattern increasingly intolerable? Is the corporate culture gradually spilling over into your 'family culture'? And so on.

A clean sheet of paper

If after completing the questionnaire, you think it's time to look elsewhere, don't just turn to the obvious alternatives: similar jobs advertised in the newspaper, or a rival company. Take a few moments to think through just what you want to be doing for the next stage of your life. Even if, at the end of the day, you decide that what you want is exactly the same job at another company, at least you'll have done so by a process of conscious choice. And you'll have a better sense of your marketability somewhere else.

The clean sheet of paper approach revolves around three guidelines: where, what and who?

Where? Where do you want to live and work? If you've vaguely thought of emigrating before (and thousands of people leave Britain for good every year), is now the time to investigate possible destinations more closely?

If you're committed to staying in Britain, are you sure you want to work where you do? Even if you like the place where you live, would you like to change your commuting pattern? If you're thinking of moving, remember that a change of house on top of a change of job makes the family disruption much greater.

Take into account quality of life indicators: what are the schools like in the place you're moving to? What are house prices like? How high is the unemployment rate? (That's important, even if you're sure of your own job once you move. Low unemployment means a better negotiating position at pay-rise times; an easier job search for your partner; and better local prospects for your children for part-time or summer jobs and eventual careers.)

What? Do you want a similar job or something very different? If your current job isn't making proper use of your skills, is that just a problem of the place in which you're currently working, or is that always likely to be the case unless you change your line of work radically? If you want to make a drastic change, you'll need to follow the 27-step guide to a new career (see page 102).

Who? What sort of company do I want to work for? Have I got anyone in mind? How large a company do I want to work for? Multinational (20,000 employees plus)? Big national company (1,000–20,000)? Medium-sized (100–1,000)? Small (0–100)? Am I looking for a small, flexible, fast-moving company? Or do I prefer the security of a more planned, orderly company? Am I looking for somewhere aggressive or somewhere friendly and relaxed? Am I looking for prestige in my employer? Or don't I care about that?

The five ages of business

Whatever you'd *like* to do depends, of course, on whatever someone's willing to *employ* you to do. That, in part, depends on where you stand in your career. No one's going to employ you as a managing director if you're 23 and still in your first job. Equally, you won't find it easy to switch to an entry-level job after the age of 33 or so – even if you can afford to accept the salary. Your options are, in large part, determined by where you stand within the business life-cycle.

Five ages of business

(*Note: All ranges overlap*)
- **Beginner** 25 or less
  Traits: learning, enthusiastic, frustrated at not getting responsibility fast enough. Bit erratic, social life very important.
  Options: everything; complete career change possible, including fresh educational start.
  Dangers: not realizing how wide options are; getting frustrated and quitting too soon.

■ **Settling down** 20–35
Traits: acquiring real depth of knowledge; eager for salary progression; torn between work and beginning of family life. Marked shift towards responsibility.
Options: still wide – for example, best time to go abroad; track record starts to define you; last chance for painless radical career change.
Dangers: not widening experience enough; letting new family responsibilities oppress you; becoming bolshy, so missing out on peak.

■ **Peak** 30–45
Traits: most productive years; family life settled; often unveil unexpected creativity; very hard work.
Options: complete career change harder; change within industry at its easiest; big salary gains possible.
Dangers: not exploiting marketability enough; allowing salary grievances to build up; not being realistic about long-term prospects.

■ **Conflict** 40–55
Traits: beware – tension builds about career; family life also changes sharply; some people go to top, others clearly on their way out.
Options: push for top; 'second phase' career aimed at family, social concerns; self-employment.
Dangers: giving up (premature 'coasting'); allowing yourself to be pushed into self-employment or dead-end job; loss of self-esteem if did not make the cut.

■ **Maturity** 50–retirement
Traits: can be very rewarding if exploit 'mentor' role; wisdom often compensates for flagging energy.
Options: starting again; self-employment; start-up or turnaround.
Dangers: can be fatal if self-esteem slides too far; important to stay in touch with younger managers or run the risk of being frozen out.

The trick is to make the most of the options at each stage.

Beginner. In this phase, remember that your options are almost infinite; don't feel trapped or moulded by what you've done so far. Of course, a really big career change may need a difficult and costly investment in education (an adult degree, an MBA, a computer course). Still, no matter how hard and expensive that may seem now, it will certainly be more difficult later on. So, if you think you're likely to need it, make the switch now. At this stage, your specific job experience may well be less important than the fact that you've been a satisfactory employee in general. So you can contemplate a less-than-complete job change without too much fear of being ignored.

Settling down. In the 20–35 age range, you're starting to be valuable for – and thus partly defined by – your specific job experience. There's still time for a drastic change, but it gets more painful with each passing year to persuade someone to take you on in an entry-level job. This is a good time to explore a career change within your company; you've built up a reasonable track record with them, but you aren't yet finally pigeon-holed. And it's also a good time to acquire international experience, while your children are still young enough to avoid school problems and you're still flexible enough to find that the challenge outweighs the inconveniences.

Peak. In this phase, it's important to make the most of your options; you're at your most creative and also most attractive (though outsiders' knowledge of you often lags a few years behind your achievements, so make sure you get a name for yourself outside your own company, if necessary, by making it yourself). A complete career change is now much harder – and certainly requires sacrificing some of the ease and authority you're starting to feel in your current job. But the good news is you can make big salary gains by exploiting your value to the company – now probably at its peak in relation to what you're paid. A careful change of employer can take you rapidly upwards in terms of salary and seniority.

Conflict. When you enter the conflict zone everything starts to happen at once. At work, new possibilities open up, but there are also worries about whether you'll be one of the relatively small number of people to step upwards in the rapidly narrowing pyramid. At home, as your children grow older life gets more complicated. And in yourself, intimations of mortality seep in, as your body starts to give the first unmistakeable signs of ageing. Whatever you do during this period, think hard about it: it's easy, under the many pressures of home and work, to make the wrong decision. And your scope for recovering from a career mistake is much less in your 40s or early 50s than it is in your 20s or 30s.

The options open to you include a determination to push on to the highest possible levels in your organization, or a recognition that, in cost-benefit terms, the chance of ultimate success is outweighed by the pain of the struggle. The people who do reach the very highest levels are often those who continue to press ahead in their 40s with as much energy and ambition as they displayed in their 20s. Others, with smaller reserves of ambition to draw on, drop by the wayside and settle for making the most of their existing achievements. That's by no means a foolish strategy, of course, because the costs of continued ambition are considerable. If you think you have only an outside chance of getting the top job you're aiming for, it may well not be worthwhile continuing to put up with the rigours of the fast track.

This gives you, paradoxically, a greater range of options than in your 'peak' years. You can continue to push for the top; shift to a 'second-phase' career which gives you more time with your family or meets your growing concern with social issues; or opt for self-employment, drawing on the experience and maturity you've acquired up till now to be your own boss.

The pitfalls are various: if you give up too soon, you may miss out on the potential rewards you've been aiming for just as they start to become attainable; you can allow yourself to be pushed prematurely into a dead-end job, or into self-employment, even though it doesn't suit you. Or you can plunge into protracted depression and self-doubt once it becomes clear that you're not one of the favoured handful who'll go on to fight for the top honours.

The key to surviving the conflict age is thought: think hard, and as realistically as possible, about your promotion chances, and think hard about what you really want out of your remaining 20 years or so of economic activity. Here's a useful test:

■ Write down the things in your life you particularly value; arrange them in order of priority, or give each of them the weighting you ascribe to their importance.

■ Now put yourself in the position of an impartial, outside observer. Look at yourself dispassionately and, from the outsider's viewpoint, write down how much time, energy and intensity you devote to those activities.

■ If the two lists are very different, reassess the priorities you listed in the first step. Were you serious about them? If you still hold to the values you put down in the first step, but the second step tells you that you aren't putting those views into practice, there's something wrong, and a possible case for rethinking what you do or how you do it.

Maturity. These years can be some of the most rewarding of your business career. At work, you have come to terms with the outcome of the struggle for the top, and are often calmer, wiser and able to offer advice and help to younger people. But you have many other options.

If your firm's pension plan allows early retirement on acceptable terms, you have, truly, the option of starting again. Using your pension money to subsidize your income, you can switch to a more lowly-paid job in a more attractive organization or region.

Because your family expenses may be past their peak and your mortgage burden is likely to be relatively light, you have much more flexibility over salaries, even if early retirement isn't an option: for example, self-employment can be less fraught than if a growing family's finances hang on every contract.

The risks, of course, are that if your importance declines at work and you don't have any offsetting social or leisure interest to fill the gap, your self-esteem and energy levels can decline too far and too fast – something that can be, in some researchers' eyes, literally fatal. And, of course, if you stay at your firm but aren't able to build close links with the younger generation of managers, you may find yourself pushed to the margins of corporate life.

Step by step: the 27-step guide to a new career
If you're serious about wanting a change of career, you have to take the process seriously; the worst thing you can do is leap at an obvious job change – an advertisement or a headhunter's call – without thinking through what is best for you to do.

Finding a new career isn't easy; it takes hard work and a fair amount of courage, particularly if you haven't been exposed to the snubs of the job market for a while. As you go through the 27 steps outlined below, try to be realistic about your own willingness to undertake the trials of job-hunting, and assess the likely outcome. (Note: being realistic doesn't always mean being pessimistic.)

Make sure you've got enough free time in the coming weeks

to do the thinking, research, letter-writing and interview-attending that the job search will require. And bear in mind that if you're serious about changing careers, the least you may have to do is sacrifice some of this year's holiday for the cause; it can't all be done in lunch-breaks and furtive phone calls from your desk.

27 steps to a new career

SELF-ASSESSMENT/RESEARCH

1. **Self-screening.** Try to answer these questions, on paper or in your head:
   - What are your strengths?
   - What are your interests?
   - What would other people say about you?
   - How hungry are you?
   - How willing are you to accept risk?
   - Are you an 'expert', or a 'manager'? Which do you prefer?
   - Are you free to plan your career, or do your family's concerns also enter into the picture (for example, spouse's job)?

2. **Objectives.** Use what you've learnt about yourself to set some general objectives. Try to give a range, from minimum to ideal:
   - Financial
   - Work demands
   - Location
   - Essential perks (for example, pension, car)

3. **What type of job.** Now try to assess the broad characteristics of the job you want. Don't pin it down to a specific industry or job title yet. Instead, ask yourself:
   - Managing or doing?
   - Big company or small?
   - Function: sales, finance, production, etc?

4. **Preliminary research.** This is the stage at which you don't make assumptions. Don't assume that certain types of job or

company are more attractive than others; try to find some facts. The Jobs Column in the *Financial Times* (every Wednesday) publishes regular salary comparisons; you can usually get fuller details from the consultants who provide them. Some trade magazines give salary details. Ask as many people as you can what job prospects in their industry are like. Systematically analyse a few weeks' job ads. Where are the jobs? What do they pay? What's involved?

5. **Focus.** Now, with some broad knowledge of the jobs market, you can start to focus on a few industries, companies or towns that appeal to you most. You'll have an idea of the span of jobs in each that meet your basic criteria. Try to make the list longer rather than shorter; you'll need as many opportunities as possible when you start writing off for jobs.

6. **Industry research.** Try to find out as much as you can about the industries you're targeting. Go to a good business or economics library and read trade magazines and specialist publications. Get the librarian to help you find past background articles in the business papers or the trade press. Call up anyone you know who works in the industry and pick their brains relentlessly. You're not just trying to establish where the best job prospects are at this stage, you're also trying to build up enough of a database to appear intelligent at an interview. Once you start actually applying, you may not have time to assemble all this background material before an interview, so do it now.

7. **Company research.** A similar effort is needed on the companies you're now starting to target. *Extel* and *McCarthy Information Services* (available at business libraries) will help you with big firms; for big and small ones go to Companies House reading rooms in London and other big cities. Company Secretaries of public companies will supply annual reports on request. And try to get any gossip from people in the companies or their rivals: corporate culture, dominant departments, etc.

8. **People research.** Who matters at these firms? Try to build up a picture of who the key managers are in the area you're

targeting. (Annual reports and the trade press are a big help here; so is industry gossip.) What are the key managers like? Do they have pet hates? Stock phrases? Are they on the way up or down? Who'll make the final hiring decision?

9. **Pause: do you really want to do this?** By now, you'll have invested considerable time and effort in the job search; you may even have told family and friends you're looking around. Don't let the momentum sweep you away. Ask yourself: Now I know more about the opportunities elsewhere, how do those in my own company look? Are there ways of achieving my objectives within my own firm? How do other companies stack up against my present employer in terms of corporate style, etc? Should I think twice before committing myself to a real job-change campaign?

SEARCH/MARKETING

10. **Basics: CV, appearance, etc.** If you're going ahead, it's time to get the basics right. Prepare a good, crisp curriculum vitae (at most two pages). Follow the outline attached to this chapter (on page 113). Make sure you've got at least two sets of presentable interview clothes and a good haircut. Unless you're an academic or a researcher, consider shaving off a beard if you have one. You can always grow it back later – and some people just hate candidates with beards. If you wear glasses, consider investing in a new pair: your old style may make you look old-fashioned. But don't choose anything daring as a replacement. Find out how successful people at the company you want to be hired by look, and try to dress as much like them as possible. Make it easy for them to think your face fits.

11. **Getting the word out.** Your best chance of finding an unadvertised job is through word of mouth. Make sure news of any opportunities reaches you by letting every acquaintance know you're looking for a job. (Give them a broad-brush idea of what you're looking for, so there won't be any nasty surprises.) Ask each person you know to pass the word on. And try to get everyone you know to funnel back job opportunities.

12. Seeking advice. This is a surprisingly effective technique for getting to see important people – and even, occasionally, for getting useful advice. Don't expect the person whose advice you're ostensibly seeking to say: 'Well, as a matter of fact, we're looking for someone just like you . . .' (though it does happen). Expect rather to get a feel for the company, to plant your face in someone's memory and to start to build up the personal links that in the long term are the most effective job-search tools.

13. Writing the letter/making the phone call. There's usually no substitute, then, for sitting down and writing a letter of application. Even if, through persistent phoning, you establish that there's a vacancy of the sort you're looking for, you'll probably still be asked for an application letter before the first interview. Remember, the CV gives your history; the letter is to say why it's particularly relevant to *this* job, in *this* company, at *this* moment. Don't undersell!

14. Toughing it out. When your first round of letters gets nowhere, don't despair. Try a polite follow-up phone call to find out what was wrong (wrong person? wrong experience? wrong timing?). Go back to the recipient in six months' time with a follow-up ('Since then I've been promoted . . . successfully completed a project . . . etc'). Try other departments in the same company. Reassess the level at which you're pitching your application (too low? too high?) and try again.

15. Lining up allies. This is worth doing *before* any interview, because there won't be time to do it afterwards. Allies include people you know inside the company, or influential suppliers or customers. You can drop their names in the interview – and they're far more effective than formal referees.

16. Interview preparation.
  ■ Find out who'll be doing the interview
  ■ Find out what's the purpose (that is, what *they* think the purpose is)

■ Get someone to do a mock interview, and practise answering the four inevitable questions: 'What do you think you can do for this company?'; 'Why do you want to leave your present employer?'; 'Why do you want the job?'; and 'What do you think your strengths and weaknesses are?' until you've got them off pat and sound sincere at the same time

17. **Initial interview.** This may be quite casual, especially if you've written in on spec and there are no specific jobs in prospect yet. Beware, though. A damning comment on your file (or a damning impression left in the head of someone influential) can be a permanent blackball. Try as hard as you can, even if the person interviewing you is the wrong one/ too junior/too senior/too bored.

18. **Getting feedback.** This is just as important as the interview. Don't hesitate to call and chat to the person who interviewed you. By now, he or she will have relaxed with you and may well be able to give you a more honest assessment of whether there's a job you're suitable for, and what the competition's like. Try to make it a relaxed chat, rather than a continuation of the interview: you'll get more information that way.

SALES/DECISION

19. **Making the short-list.** This is probably the most crucial moment, so it's worth bringing everything you can to bear on it. Mobilize your supporters. Send round any additional information that is relevant to the subjects touched on in the interview (this will give you an opportunity to do a bit more selling of yourself in the covering letter). Keep in touch by phone with whoever will be drawing up the short-list, trying to create the sort of bonds that will make it hard for them to cross you off.

20. **Selling yourself to the boss.** Once you're past the first stages, a different set of skills will be necessary when selling yourself to the boss. Try to get the past interviewers (and anyone else you know) to give you an idea of what the

boss's view of the job is (as opposed to everyone else's). Try
to present yourself as a long-term additional plus for the
company, not just a lump of costs who happens to meet a
short-term need. Sell yourself as someone who fits in with
the firm's real goals (see page 40).

21. **The bargaining begins.** Once you're a (or, ideally, *the*)
favoured candidate, you have to make the difficult switch
from supplicant to negotiator – particularly tricky if you
wrote in out of the blue. Key things to remember:
   - Once they've made an emotional commitment to choosing
     you, they won't be easily dissuaded, so you've probably
     got more leverage than you think
   - It's important to make your requirements clear in one go,
     rather than springing extra demands on them late in the
     process. That may well work (because of the emotional
     commitment), but it will cloud your arrival

22. **Doing the deal.** Don't be carried away by your desire to
join the company. Get a good deal-making handbook, and
negotiate till you've got an acceptable compromise on your
objectives. Are you above the minimum second step (on
page 102)?

23. **Audit what you're offered.** Before you finally accept,
make sure you know exactly what's on the table. I once
ended up with a ten per cent pay-cut (and a long-lasting
sense of grievance) because I misunderstood how much
money I was being offered. It takes a special kind of
foolishness to do that – but it's much more common to be
confused about pensions, bonuses, profit-sharing, cars and
other perks. Get them to spell out the details, and try to
calculate a total value for the package. Then do the same
thing for your current employment, so you can compare.

24. **Playing one off against the other.** Life normally ensures
that, after months of fruitless search, you'll ultimately be
deluged with offers, all with pressing deadlines for
acceptance. Take your time: people rarely have the sort of
urgency they claim, and if they want you enough to offer
you the job, they'll wait for you to ponder it. Try not to leave
people hanging, though: set a reasonable deadline for a

decision (say, seven to ten days' time) and stick to it. Then hustle to get a firm offer out of the rival, making it clear you've got an alternative offer. You can usually use rival offers to prise a bit more money out of your preferred company – but the best time of all to be in demand is in the closing stages of the interview process, when a rival bidder makes you seem much more attractive, and eases the switch from supplicant to bargainer.

25. **Pause: do I really want to do this?** Do I? How much more money will I get than in my present job, after allowing for all perks (the new company's bonuses always seem greener)? Will I meet my objectives? How far does the job really match up with the profile I drew up in Step 1? If you don't like the answer to any of these questions, say no, politely. And if you're uncertain, ask to see the person you'll be directly working for again, to talk through the issues. Don't let the momentum carry you away. An employer would far rather you quit three days before you join than three months after.

26. **Leaving your old job gracefully.** You may want (or need) to come back. So be polite. Don't make the farewell speech you've always promised yourself. Smile politely when people you can't stand give you farewell gifts you can't bear. Try to clear things up for your successor and pass on a few (not too many) tips of the trade. But *do* try to get away as early as humanly possible: those long-drawn-out three month notice periods are very tough. Your heart's not in the job, and your bosses have no compunction about loading you up with unpleasant tasks in the last few weeks.

27. **Arriving well.** Turn up when you said you would. Make a good impression. If you're the new boss, try to project an image of decisiveness and authority: your ability to get things done will never be greater than in the first six weeks, when people *expect* change. If you let things linger on without changes beyond that, you're implicitly endorsing the *status quo*, and will have that much more trouble making changes later. Any mistakes you make from lack of knowledge will be forgiven because you're new. And

anyway, you may be able to see things more clearly than if you were bogged down in detail.

If you're not the boss, lie low and listen for a week or so, then gradually start to make a contribution, build up alliances and participate. Try to pick up as much history as you can during the period in which people will forgive you for not knowing it. Later on, it'll be harder to ask: 'Why exactly do we all hate marketing?'

And congratulations: you've made what you know will be a wise move.

Who should and who shouldn't consider setting up on their own

If your career is stalled, or you just can't bear being a cog in a machine any longer, self-employment – running a small business, or setting up as a freelance or consultant – may seem very attractive. Sometimes it is; often, fundamental problems of economics or temperament doom such ventures from the outset. There are some simple guidelines to help tell who should, and who shouldn't consider setting up on their own.

- *How much do you know about the business you're about to enter?* The best single indicator of success in a new venture is deep past experience in the field. So starting up your own restaurant or wool shop, no matter how badly you think the village needs one, is a bad way to begin if all your previous experience has been as a research chemist. If you are determined to set up on your own, try very hard to find a business you're already very familiar with (and not just as a customer). That's a much better bet than ploughing the life savings into a hotel or a shop: two common routes to failure.
- *Have you been prepared to get your feet wet first?* Another important indicator of success is an attempt to set the business up – successfully, but

on a small scale – in your spare time. Some venture capitalists won't invest in people who haven't tried this. After all, if you haven't got the determination and strength of character to give up your weekends and evenings to an experimental venture, you're scarcely likely to be able to cope with the 100 per cent commitment required by your own small business. If you find yourself saying: 'Of course, I can't do anything till I've given up my job', that's probably an indication that you aren't really cut out for self-employment. Apart from anything else, a small-scale pilot will give you a chance to get real customer reaction – something that's more valuable than all the neatly-typed business plans in the world.

■ *Can you cope with commercial realities?* A lot of people think that because they work in business, they could run their own. Wrong. Almost everyone who works for a company with more than 20 people is insulated from some of the nastiness of life in small business. How much patience have you got for organizing the photocopier? Logging overdue debtors – and phoning them (politely) every day until they pay up? Cold calling for customers? Haggling with suppliers? And so on. If you're a big-company expert thinking of becoming a consultant, you may be especially vulnerable. If you haven't got a background of *ad hoc* commercial enterprise, ask yourself carefully not only *can* I do all these unpleasant tasks, but also do I really *want* to? Find someone who has already followed the same path, and ask them what it's like.

■ *Are you estimating your revenues correctly?* People are normally fairly good at estimating the costs of their new venture – it's what they spend most of their time calculating, after all, once the original idea strikes. They spend proportionately far less time on getting an accurate estimate of revenues, and are correspondingly far less good at it. So resolve to spend as much time as possible on estimating revenues. Ask comparable firms; do some quick and dirty market research. Find a friendly expert and bounce your revenue projections off him or her to see if he or she laughs. And allow for recession – make sure you can survive with a 'low' revenue estimate that's at least 33 per cent below your best guess of the outcome. (Note: if you find yourself getting bored while researching and estimating revenue, that's another warning sign, because you'll certainly find yourself doing it over and over again in the years ahead.)

■ *Have you calculated a proper cash-flow forecast?* And have you got enough capital to survive it? Most of the 'start your own business' books tell you how to calculate a cash-flow forecast, but until you start up in business for yourself you won't appreciate just how vital it is. People in large companies are usually completely insulated from cash flow, except as a concept in esoteric investment planning tools. When you've got a small business to run, cash flow takes on a whole other meaning. Until you've watched your overdraft creeping remorselessly towards its unbreakable limit, with still no sign of the long-promised cheque from your best (but irredeemably tardy) customer, Megacorp Plc, you don't quite get the point. Remember, the aggressive cash management your financial director used to boast about, when you were working for Megacorp yourself, is largely directed at companies without enough clout to insist on speedy payment – which means small businesses like you. So calculate a nice, conservative cash-flow forecast, then lag all revenues by three months and see what happens to the business. Then add in some bad news (a recession; a debtor going bankrupt; ten per cent wage inflation, but only a five per cent price rise; a 15 per cent sterling revaluation; and so on) and see if the lagged cash flow can keep you afloat. If you find this exercise a bit upsetting, you may not have the stomach for setting up on your own after all.

Conclusion

Protecting your career is never easy; in a recession it's harder still. The most important ingredient is *thought*: not letting your career drift on as the net result of other people's ambitions; trying to plan clearly what you want out of life, assessing, as coolly as you can, the options open to you at each stage of your working life; and putting time and reflection into the process of changing jobs or setting up on your own.

A recession doesn't prevent you from doing any of these things; it may even open up unexpected opportunities. But before you jump at them, make sure you sit down with a sheet of paper and a pencil to work through the checklists in this chapter.

OUTLINE CV

Your name
Address

Phone numbers
Employment

    19xx– Name of current employer, abbreviated address
    Job title
    Activities, scope of responsibility, successes

    19xx–xx Penultimate employer, abbreviated address
    Job title
    Activities, scope of responsibility, successes

    ... and so on. If your career is well developed, you may want to summarize a few early jobs, thus:

    19xx–xx Various jobs as xxx. Employers included: xxx, xxx, xxx. Duties included: xxx, xxx, xxx

    Don't use this for more than two to three years, or it will look as if you're trying to hide something.

Education
How much detail you give under this heading depends on how far it is behind you. If you are at the beginning of your career, put this section first, and leave summer or part-time jobs till later. Similarly, if you've just acquired a new educational qualification, put the education section first, to impress your new status in the minds of potential employers.

Someone in mid-career should summarize education thus:

19xx–xx	Tadcaster Polytechnic
	BSc in Food Technology
19xx–xx	Tadcaster High School
	2 A-levels, 6 O-levels

No further detail is required, though if you got a First or Upper 2nd Class Degree, you should mention it. Do not go into details about school examinations unless they're all you've got to show and you're still very young.

Other abilities
Fluent French, rusty German
Competent with Lotus 1-2-3

Do not mention hobbies or athletic achievements (unless you can say something like 'represented UK in the Olympic Games').

STEP 4

Salvaging the Family Finances

It helps to think of your family as a small business. That doesn't mean you should be planning to send the children up the chimney or turn the back garden into a turnip field; but it does mean that when you start the task of protecting the household finances against the impact of recession, there are a number of ways in which thinking like a managing director rather than a parent can help.

First, family finances are now as complicated as those of a small business. In the good old days of a single bread-winner and a largely cash-based existence, household money flows were simple. The family balance sheet was simple, too: a house on the asset side, perhaps, with a mortgage on the other; perhaps a bit of hire purchase. Now, with credit cards, house equity loans, multiple income streams, many more regular outgoings (such as health insurance) than before, the picture is far more complicated. Too complicated to keep in your head. But we still tend to think of family finances as something we can keep in our heads, or at least on the back of a gas bill envelope. You wouldn't try to keep a small business's financial operations on the back of an envelope, though. If thinking of the household as a small business is enough to get you to write things down more explicitly, it has served its main purpose.

Second, families, like businesses, need to plan ahead. The concept of a 'growth company' has, since the 1950s, made every professionally-managed business conscious of the need to look at least a year ahead at revenues, costs, major investments and the timing of cash flows. Doing that, even in outline form, will make it easier to cope with a recession once it's on the horizon.

Third, inflation-proofing is something companies have learnt how to do the hard way. Families did, too, in the 1970s. In the 1980s, however, with low, not-too-volatile inflation and substantial real income gains for those in work, families have eased their inflation vigilance. Companies haven't; and a bit of that wariness should rub off on you at home. Just as in the 1970s, it won't be good enough to think complacently that you're earning more this year than you did last; the crucial question is: How much have costs risen in the same period? And not just anybody's costs (expressed in the Retail Prices Index). *Your* costs, expressed in the gas bill and the phone bill and the supermarket bill.

Fourth, thinking of your family as a small business also helps to drive home the unpredictability of economic life. Again, for those in work, the late 1980s bred a false sense of security: each year, incomes went up and family wealth went up too. Because much of family life is crushingly predictable – same house, same kids, same type of car, same holidays – it's easy to forget that economic conditions are much more volatile than that. A small business has much more unpredictable revenue and costs, and profits are chancier. Thinking like a small business manager, rather than a bread-winner, helps to keep you on your toes about what could go wrong.

Because a lot *could* go wrong. A sharp recession coupled with inflation and stagnant or falling house prices could hit all parts of a family's finances simultaneously. The more you've thought about the year ahead, the better prepared you'll be to cope with such an unpleasant development when it happens.

That's why the first half of this chapter focuses on establishing where your finances are now and how they'll look over the next 12 months. Only when you've got a handle on that can you move on to the more ambitious task of protecting them against what the future might bring.

Assessing where you stand

Your household finances have three components:

- Income and outgoings (the 'profit and loss account' of your notional small business).
- Assets and liabilities (the 'balance sheet').
- Cash flow (which is what it sounds like).

The worksheet below will allow you to estimate all these components. Before you start to fill it in, remember that it is intended to provide a sort of 'steady state' view of your finances; we'll come to the part where we project the future later on. But it is easiest to think of your household finances on an annualized basis. So assume that, for the next 12 months, the pattern of income and outgoings remains as it is. Unless your next pay-rise is imminent (ie, in the next month) don't include it. Equally, if your spouse does a bit of temporary work around Christmas time, only include a few weeks' worth of income in the calculations.

Where you stand: a family worksheet

Income

1 Salary A
  (after tax, National Insurance and pension contribution)
2 Salary B
  (after tax, National Insurance and pension contribution)
3 Other salaries
  (after tax, National Insurance and pension contribution)
4 Freelance earnings A
  (net of expenses)
5 Freelance earnings B
  (net of expenses)

6 Other freelance earnings
7 Dividends
8 Bank/building society interest received
9 National Savings interest received
10 Other income

Total

Outgoings

11 Mortgage
12 Endowment insurance (if any)
13 House insurance
14 Contents insurance
15 Other life insurance (if any)
16 Health insurance
17 Community charge ('poll tax')
   (multiply figure for your council by number of adults)
18 Water
   (multiply quarterly bills by four to get annual figure)
19 Telephone
   (as for water)
20 Electricity
   (as for water, but allow for winter/summer difference)
21 Gas
   (as for electricity)
22 Central heating oil
23 Milk
   (weekly bill × 52)
24 Newspapers and books
   (weekly bill + purchases of magazines and books × 52)
25 Food
   (weekly supermarket shopping + however much you spend at local shops, all × 52. Also add in sweets and alcohol bought from off-license)

26 Clothes A
(try to estimate an annual figure)
27 Clothes B
28 Children's and other clothes
29 Travel to work/school
(eg, monthly season × 12)
30 Meals during working hours and school meals
(weekly figure × 52)
31 Petrol
(eg, tankfuls per month × size of tank × petrol price × 12)
32 Children's pocket money
33 School or other fees
(eg, piano lessons, school trips)
34 Child care
(nursery fees, nanny's wages, child-minding fees, *au pair* payments, etc)
35 Presents, cards, postage and other stationery
(weekly figure × 52)
36 Holidays
(yearly: includes fares, hotels and out-of-pocket spending)
37 Entertainment
(monthly × 12; includes pub spending, video rental, etc)
38 Eating out
(monthly figure × 12)
39 Hire-purchase payments on past purchases
40 Credit-card payments
(interest and paying off of past credit-card balances)
41 Purchase or replacement of small household equipment
(kitchenware, records, pictures, etc)
42 DIY goods and tools
43 Rental of equipment (eg, television)
44 Purchase of consumer durables
(estimate for the year ahead, if you will pay for them out of income; if you expect to borrow to buy them, include the monthly payments on the appropriate line)

Total

Subtract this total from the total income figure calculated above. Result is:
End-year surplus/deficit:

Assets

100 House
   (a conservative estimate, based on the last sale of a house near you. Try to avoid taking the asking price as gospel!)
101 Endowment policy
   (encashment value of – but see next chapter)
102 Other life insurance policies
   (encashment values)
103 Car
   (look up value in second-hand car magazine)
104 Consumer durables
   (see separate worksheet, opposite)
105 Investments, savings accounts, etc for A
   (include gold if any)
106 Investments, savings accounts, etc for B
   (include gold if any)
107 Investments, savings accounts, etc for others
   (include gold if any)
108 Current accounts: positive balances

Total Liabilities

109 Mortgage
110 HP debt outstanding
111 Car loan
112 Loans from employers (excluding season ticket loan)
113 Overdraft
114 Balance on credit cards

Total

Subtract total liabilities from total assets to get:
Net worth:

Consumer durable worksheet. If you have a lot of consumer durables, it is worth calculating their depreciated value. This will enable you to keep track of how much any delay in replacing them is affecting your overall household net worth. If you want to do this, use the worksheet below. If it's more trouble than it's worth, make a rough overall estimate and allow for the fact that the fridge is worth less now than when you bought it (especially since the kids scratched their initials on the door).

	Purchase price	*Age*	*Current value*
TV			
Video-recorder			
Other video equip			
Stereo equipment			
Washing machine			
Drier			
Dishwasher			
Computer			
Vacuum cleaner			
Refrigerator			
Oven			
Hob			
Microwave oven			

To calculate the current value of each of these things, assume they have a five-year life. If they're in the first year, they're worth 100 per cent of their purchase price; if they're five years old, they're worth zero. In year two, consequently, they're worth 80 per cent, in year three 60 per cent, in year four 20 per cent and in year five, zero.

If you expect to re-do your kitchen regularly, do the same calculation based on the cost of kitchen refurbishment and the number of years you expect the kitchen to last

What it's all for? These worksheets may seem formidable, but they shouldn't take more than a few hours to calculate if you are prepared to do some guesstimating for the numbers that are hard to find. Once you've done them you'll know:

- Whether, as things stand, you're able to cover your outgoings.
- How much, notionally, you're worth. This figure is not much by itself, but it will be extremely useful in a moment when we come to calculate how things will look in a year's time.

But the real value of the numbers is as a baseline from which to calculate the impact of any bad times.

Projecting the future

The last few pages of calculations will have given you a 'steady state' calculation of your income, outgoings and net worth. Time now to project them forwards – first on a steady state basis, then allowing for the impact of bad times.

Start by taking your current net worth, as shown above. Then adjust for changes in the year ahead: the consumer durables you intend to buy, the HP you plan to take on to finance them and the net surplus or deficit from the income and outgoings calculation you did first of all. Thus:

Net assets now:
Add: change of value of house (careful!):
Add: surplus or deficit on income/outgoings:

Add: asset purchases net of incremental debt:
Subtract: depreciation on consumer durables for year ahead:

The total is:
Projected net worth a year hence:

By subtracting from this the original net worth calculation you
can reach:
Projected change in net worth:

Right away this calculation will show you whether you're
likely to be better or worse off at the end of the year; and if the
answer is 'worse', you should take some of the steps outlined in
this chapter even if you don't really think there will be a
recession.

The true value of the calculation, however, is as a basis from
which to measure the impact of a recession. Here's how to do
it.

Assessing the impact of recession and inflation. Start by
writing down a number of the calculations you've made
earlier:

1 Total income:
2 Total outgoings:
3 Mortgage payments:
4 House value:
5 Net worth at the beginning of the year:
6 Projected net worth at the end of the year:

Now start filling in numbers in answer to these questions:

If there's a recession, and the company's profits are
threatened, how big a pay-rise do you think you will get
this year? (If more than one person in the household goes

out to work, estimate a combined figure that reflects the comparative importance of the salaries.)
7 Projected pay-rise (%):

What is inflation likely to be this year? (Find a consensus figure from a newspaper: the figure you want is the 'underlying' rate, which excludes mortgage interest.)
8 Inflation forecast:

Will there be other ill-effects (for example, reduced overtime, lower bonus)? If yes, subtract reductions for both you and your partner from total income and write the new figure here; if no, write the total income figure shown above here:
9 Adjusted total income:

Allow for a further rise in interest rates. Divide your mortgage payments by the current interest rate and multiply by an interest rate one percentage point higher.
10 Mortgage payment after increase:

Allow for a 20 per cent fall in house prices. Take the start-of-the-year value of your home and multiply by 0.2.
11 Drop in house value:

Now take answer 9, adjusted income, and multiply by answer 7, projected pay-rise, to give:
12 Income after inflation:

Subtract your mortgage payments, answer 3, from total outgoings, answer 2, and multiply the result by the inflation rate. Add answer 10, mortgage payment after increase, to give:
13 Outgoings after inflation and mortgage rate rise:

Subtract the new outgoings figure, answer 11, from income after inflation, answer 10. This gives you:

14 Surplus/deficit on income and outgoings for year ahead (after allowing for inflation):

Subtract this surplus/deficit figure from projected end-year net worth, answer 6, and subtract drop in house value, answer 11, also.

15 *Adjusted net worth:*

Compare this with the end-year net worth figure you projected originally.

To assess the impact of more serious economic problems, simply raise the inflation rate and the interest rate in these calculations, and reduce the income further (in answer 9) by assuming that one member of the household loses their job. If you think my estimates of possible interest-rate rises and house-price changes are implausible, simply adjust that part of the calculations.

Note that these are quite crude calculations. They do not make an allowance for timing of pay-rises and inflation; and they do not allow for actions you may take in reaction to all the bad news this exercise assumes.

And I will cheerfully admit to one big implausibility. The calculations assume you can automatically finance any size of deficit on the income and outgoings calculation (answer 14). In fact, of course, though building societies will go some way to help troubled mortgage-borrowers, most lending institutions are unlikely to extend you unlimited credit. You would have to stop running up that deficit at some point and take alternative action.

The calculations do, however, give you some idea about just how serious this problem might be. If there *is* a deficit on the income/outgoings statement under any scenario, you will need to finance it by liquidating some of your assets or borrowing. The two different calculations of the surplus/deficit – the steady state original, and the new, adjusted one in answer 14 – show how that financing need increases rapidly as the economy deteriorates.

Taking steps now to cope with the worst

Now that you know how bad things could be if the economy starts to worsen, it's time to start turning those gloomy thoughts into action.

It's not necessary to make complete preparations for the very worst now. It would help, though, to know what steps you would take if the worst actually came about – if you or your partner lost your job, for example.

And, more practically, there are things you can start doing now to prepare for a less devastating piece of bad news – a sharp drop in your purchasing power and net wealth.

The steps I'm recommending fall into three categories: things to do now; things to do if the very worst takes place; and things to do if something unpleasant but less overwhelming happens. First, things to do now:

Turn those calculations into a practical budget. For this, you'll need the income and outgoings from your 'steady state' calculations. Try to even out your outgoings from month to month as far as possible by making use of the monthly-payment plans offered by people like electricity, gas and insurance providers. That will give you a list of standing orders as long as your arm, but it will mean that you can calculate month-to-month payments more predictably.

The budget will look like this:

Regular standing orders or direct debits	£00.00
Regular cash payments (paper bill, food, etc)	£00.00
'Discretionary' cash spending	£00.00

Budgeted spending on lumpier items (clothing,
holidays, etc)   £00.00
Total budgeted spending   £00.00

There is no point in trying to follow a really detailed item-
by-item budget unless you're a numbers enthusiast; for most
people it will be such hard work that you'll feel the need to
reward yourself with a spending binge each time you do the
calculations.

Much better is to concentrate on three things:

1. **Making sure the regular cash payments aren't
   creeping up,** through such temptations as the extra bottle of
   wine every week at the supermarket, the glossy magazines
   added to the paper bill, and so on.

2. **Keeping a firm handle on the 'discretionary' cash
   spending.** Some of this isn't really discretionary – it includes
   lunches at work, for example. But it's discretionary enough to
   keep a firm hold on: eating regularly at the pub rather than the
   canteen can cost £500 a year. That's fine if you know you're
   spending it and want to do so. But if you'd really rather, on
   reflection, have the money and live with the canteen cabbage,
   it's time to take action.
      If you find you're bad at controlling this form of household
   spending, draw it out in cash once a month, divide it up into
   four weekly envelopes, and tell yourself each packet really has
   to last you the week.

3. **Keeping tabs on the running total of lumpier
   spending.** This will make sure you haven't spent all the
   holiday money by Spring, or blown the back-to-school
   clothing budget by July. Simply the knowledge that you've
   got a budget helps to control spending on these items. You
   can reinforce the message by setting up a standing order to
   transfer a regular monthly holiday payment from your current
   account to a high-interest bank or building society account.

Reduce the cost of borrowing. Look at your borrowings. Can they be reduced? Can they be financed more cheaply? Force yourself to look at Table 4, which shows the true cost of borrowing from various sources. The numbers date from early 1990, but the important thing to notice is not so much the precise rates but the remarkable difference between them.

Table 4 Cost of borrowing

Type of borrowing	*APR %**
Store credit cards	38.4
Overdraft (unauthorized)	36.0
Bank credit cards	29.8
Personal loan (unsecured)	24.9
Overdraft (authorized)	24.5
Secured loan	18.4
Mortgage	17.0

Source Blay's MoneyMakers
Note *APR is a government-mandated calculation of the 'true' interest rate on a loan

If you've each got a handful of credit cards, you could easily have £5,000 worth of borrowing outstanding that you're only vaguely aware of – let alone the car HP or the loan for the new fridge you took out because you were up against your card limit.

The monthly interest on £5,000 of credit-card bills could be anything up to £130, depending on what proportion is on store cards and what proportion is on the relatively cheaper bank cards. An extra £5,000 on a mortgage would cost only £70 in interest.

In terms of cash flow, the comparison is even steeper. You have to pay off five per cent of a credit-card balance each month; but a 30-year mortgage requires you to pay off an average of only 3.33 per cent of the capital each year.

The biggest savings, obviously, come from increasing your mortgage to pay off your credit-card bills (as long as you then make sure you keep your credit-card balances at zero). But even without such an elaborate undertaking, you can still make significant savings by moving down the table. Bank foyers are stuffed with glossy brochures for every conceivable type of loan at every conceivable interest rate. If you collect an armful and go through looking for the ones with the lowest APRs, you could make a significant impact on your borrowing costs – as long as you can discipline yourself to hold down the credit-card balances once you've wiped them out.

Look at the bottom line. If you think of your household as a small business, you can calculate (as in the worksheet on page 120) a surplus or deficit for the year. That is the amount by which the year's income exceeds (or falls short of) the year's outgoings. If you're not achieving a surplus, you are running down your overall wealth, and you should probably be thinking of trying to raise income or lower expenses.

But even if you *are* achieving a surplus, you should ask yourself if it's big enough. To give yourself financial autonomy – and to guard against disaster – you should probably be achieving a surplus of about five per cent of your pre-tax household income every year.

That may not sound like a lot, but for a family with a combined income of £25,000, it amounts to about £100 a month in savings over and above the money put aside for holidays, Christmas presents, and so on.

At the depths of a recession, or when inflation is forcing you to run ever faster to stand still, that may not be possible. But as you attempt to prepare for the bad times, you should set yourself a savings target of that order, and adjust life accordingly.

To achieve this surplus, you may have to try to cut household expenses. Again, thinking of the family as a small business helps; the corporate cost-cutting principles outlined in Step 2 (page 72) apply to family expenses too:

- Try a few big savings, with the aim of slashing an important component of your household expenses by 30–50 per cent (by reducing your borrowing costs, as outlined earlier, for example, or settling for a less ambitious holiday or car).
- On other items, try to hold down costs by a smaller, fixed percentage, perhaps seven to ten per cent, using your budget (and the cash-in-an-envelope approach, if necessary) to hold spending down to the levels you've set.

Assess your investment in human capital. In the long run, as any business executive knows, holding down costs is only part of the story. Far more important is ensuring long-term growth in revenues – in this case, of household incomes. Achieving sustained growth in real, after-tax income is particularly hard in a recession.

One possible preparatory step you can take is to raise your long-term earning potential (or that of your partner) by investing in personal development. The most obvious form of investment in human capital is in formal education.

- Should you spend time and money acquiring another qualification, from A-level maths to a diploma in computer science?
- Would the family benefit in the long run from scrimping to put one of its members through a mature student's degree course?
- Would formal polytechnic training in catering give your lifelong ambition of running a pub/restaurant a firmer foundation of expertise? And so on.

There are other, less obvious forms of investment in human capital: evening classes in a foreign language, for example, or spare time self-teaching of computer programming. In these cases, the main expenditure is not so much money as free time.

At all events, while you're considering how to protect yourself against recession and how to enhance your ability to prosper whether the times are bad or good, you should be considering investment to increase your long-term earning power as an integral part of your approach.

Building a contingency plan

Preparations should include having a fairly clear idea of what you would do if the clouds on the horizon suddenly turned thunderous. How would you protect your living standards in these two sets of circumstances:

- If the family's real living standards were sharply squeezed by the combination of inflation and recession.
- If something really nasty happened to the family finances – a true disaster like sustained unemployment or a really severe cutback in commission earnings.

In either case, you should have a set of options to carry out. Thinking them through in advance – maybe even costing them out and putting them down on paper – would go a long way to protect you against one of the biggest dangers to avoid when bad times strike: shocked inactivity.

You can let valuable time slip through your fingers if you haven't got a semi-automatic path to follow in those first few difficult weeks after the bad news strikes home.

Preparing for bad news

1. **Think of cuts ahead of time.** These are more serious than the mild economies outlined earlier: they include cancelling the holiday altogether, not just scaling it back; or selling the car, not just keeping it a year longer. (Remember that there will be some costs that offset a small part of the gain – the food you eat while you're at home on holiday, the bus and train fares to get to work if you've sold the car.)

2. **Think of possible ways of raising extra money.** These could be part-time or weekend jobs, freelance work, and so on. Keep an eye open for possible openings so you'll know where to start looking if you had to; think through how you'd sell yourself and what you'd hope to charge; perhaps do a bit of work on an experimental basis to work out how quickly you can perform freelance tasks and to establish yourself in the appropriate market.

3. **Make sure you could avoid a short-term cash crunch.** Learn whether you'd be able to re-finance your short-term debts, perhaps by taking out an extra mortgage. Find out what your mortgage lender's approach to people in difficulties is. Find out whether your employer makes personal loans to its staff, and what the conditions are. It will take a while – perhaps a couple of months – before you could cut expenses and raise extra income; and in the meantime it's important to keep cash flowing and preserve your creditworthiness.

In the second set of circumstances, a complete financial disaster, you'll need more help than this book can give. Prepare in advance, however, by learning enough about your company's redundancy policies and the state National Insurance and Social Security systems to have some idea of what any period of unemployment would involve. Try to think through, also, a few steps you might have to put into effect if things slid off the cliff-edge.

Disaster measures

1. **Selling the house.** Could you make do with a smaller house, or one in a less attractive area, if by doing so you'd be able to eliminate your mortgage or free some capital to get you by? Are there cheaper houses that would allow you to continue your normal pattern of activity (children going to the same schools, other adults continuing their jobs)? How much would you *really* get for your house in current market conditions, and how quickly could you sell? What are the other costs involved (estate agents, legal fees, stamp duty, moving, essential redecoration)?

2. **Changing direction.** If you were made redundant, how easy would it be for you to get a new job at a satisfactory salary in your current line of work? Should you consider a major career change to a field where jobs are easier to get? What steps should you take now to prepare yourself for such a shift if it became necessary (for example, finding out a bit more about the required qualifications, potential employers, age constraints, and so on)?

3. **Going solo.** If you lost your job, would you want to consider starting your own business? What would the economics of self-employment be like? How much would you have to charge for your services, how many jobs a week, month or year would you need to get by? Do you have the temperament for your own business (see page 109)? Could you prepare now by doing some part-time work to get yourself a name and a bit of relevant experience? What would be the absolute minimum launch costs, and how could you raise the money?

In either of these sets of circumstances – a serious squeeze or a real financial disaster – things would not be easy. With luck, even if the recession is a bad one, you'll never have to carry out the steps of the last few pages. But a few minutes spent thinking about the problems and potential solutions now, will pay off many times over if the worst did happen – and greatly add to your confidence that you can cope with disaster.

Lessening the pain of the big expenses

Big, costly lumps of household spending – holidays, work on the house, school fees, unexpected car repairs, family emergencies – are never easy to cope with. Even when the economy's booming and your earnings are at their peak, you'll still be stretched to meet a big bill, especially if it's an unexpected one. The strain is all the greater if incomes are squeezed by inflation or recession. This section describes some ways to ease the pain.

Predictable expenses. These include such regular lumps of costs as holidays, school fees or expeditions, and the costs of Christmas presents and celebrations. When times are good, you can often pay these out of income, cutting back temporarily on other expenses and allowing your overdraft or credit-card balances to take any extra strain.

When times are bad, that's much harder. You'll have less financial elbow-room when the bills come in, and you may be right up against your borrowing limits.

Ways of paying for predictable expenses

1. **'Cash in the envelope'.** Force yourself to save up for expenses you know about by putting money aside every month – perhaps literally in an envelope, but better on almost every count by opening a separate building society high-interest account and resolutely putting into it a regular sum of money (plus any unexpected windfalls). Putting money aside separately in this way not only makes it psychologically harder to break into the nest-egg for normal expenses, but also lets you create a self-reinforcing ritual. Once you've done it a few times, you'll want to continue, and the special trip to the building society to pay the money in will come to seem a virtuous ceremony, not just a wearisome task.

2. **Earn special money.** A similar psychological effect can be harnessed by dedicating overtime or part-time work to the purpose you're saving for. It's hard to psych yourself up for

overtime on a Saturday when you'd much rather be playing with the kids or watching football. The task is made a bit more palatable by the thought that the money won't simply be vanishing into the gaping maw of household expenses but will go to some special and desirable end, such as a holiday or Christmas presents for the children.

Unpredictable expenses. These include such variously random disasters as a problem with the roof, a seized-up car engine or a serious family sickness that starts costing money (either for private care, for example, for old people, or because it prevents a family member from earning their normal salary). Insurance aside, there are a number of steps you can take to ward off the worst:

Coping with expenses that come out of the blue

1. **Making the unpredictable predictable.** If you suspect your roof is going to go some time in the next year or so, build a maintenance lump sum into your yearly budget, and get it done on schedule. Similarly for a car: set aside a lump sum for repairs. Take out maintenance contracts on items of household machinery, like the central heating boiler or the washing machine; replace the car often enough to avoid unexpected repair bills; sign up for extended guarantees where possible. These all cost money, but if you're the sort of family that can cope with regular payments better than sudden emergencies, they may prove worthwhile.

2. **Have a borrowing emergency plan.** Make sure you've got access to a line of credit (from a bank, for example, or on a credit card) that you can activate immediately. Then, as soon as possible, replace that borrowing with something that takes longer to arrange but charges a lower rate of interest, such as a larger mortgage. Don't count on remortgaging your house in a hurry: no matter what the banks and building societies say, there's a good chance it will take several months – far too long to allow you to use it for an emergency.

3. **Earmark an asset for sale.** Keep at the back of your mind an asset that you could liquidate if you needed money quickly: some shares or other securities, an antique, grandfather's gold watch, some under-used sporting gear. With luck, you'll never need to turn them into cash (and, if you're unlucky, you won't get anything like what you paid for them), but having them available as a back-up will make you much calmer in coping with the emergency and negotiating with a potential lender.

The bottom line

Managing the family finances isn't easy under any circumstances; managing them when recession and inflation are both all-too-visible threats is a real challenge.

The keys to success outlined in this chapter can be summed up in three messages:

- Getting your finances on an even keel now is probably more important than any amount of planning for the future.
- Managing the family finances takes time and discipline: drawing up budgets, filing documents close to hand, keeping track of bank accounts.
- Having a mental contingency plan to cope with a sudden financial crisis could make all the difference between a controlled reduction of household spending and an abrupt, panicky descent into chaos.

Your income and outgoings, the subject of this chapter, are only part of the financial picture, however. Just as important is the overall pattern of your assets and liabilities: your wealth. Read on to the next chapter, Step 5, to tackle the question of protecting your wealth against the forces that threaten it.

STEP 5

Protecting Your Assets: Investments, Savings, Home

As well as ensuring a steady – and, if all goes well – growing flow of family income, you must also keep your eye on the value of your household assets. In inflationary times, or when house prices are fluctuating, changes in the value of your assets can have a far more dramatic impact on your family's overall financial wealth than any changes in income.

If you don't believe me, just do this calculation. Assume you're a family spending all your household income of £35,000 a year and a £40,000 mortgage on a house worth £60,000. Inflation, overall, is low – perhaps five per cent. Your household income goes up a bit more than that, perhaps seven per cent. Assuming you continue to buy the same volume of goods and services as you did last year, and there's no change in the tax rate, the amount you'll be able to add to your savings – or use to improve your standard of living – is £700. So a respectable real wage increase has added only £700 to your total assets. Meanwhile, though, house prices rocket – taking the value of your house to £100,000. That has added a notional £40,000 to your total assets – over 50 times greater than the rise in assets produced by living within your means and earning higher pay in real terms.

Now suppose that times turn bad. Inflation rises, and you can't get a pay-rise big enough to keep up with it. After last year's pay-rise, your household income is £37,450 a year. This year you get only a five per cent pay-rise on top of that, while prices rise by eight per cent. At the end of the year, to meet the same household expenses in real terms, you'll have to run down your savings by £368, or find economies of that amount. Meanwhile, house prices have slipped back, despite inflation, and your house is worth only £80,000. On paper, anyway, your net wealth has dropped by a total of £20,368, but 98.2 per cent of that drop is attributable to the swing in house prices, and only 1.8 per cent to the fact that your income hasn't kept pace with inflation.

Of course, as every pub or coffee morning conversation sagely concludes, such savings in asset values don't mean a great deal to the average family, since they have to live somewhere, and moving into rented accommodation is scarcely a realistic option in Britain.

But that piece of folk wisdom is true only up to a point. When you die, you don't have to live anywhere and your grieving heirs can sell off the house for whatever it is worth at the time. If part of your financial goal is to leave a sum of money to your children (as it is for many people), then the fluctuating value of your house or other assets is of vital importance to achieving that goal.

Less morbidly, you can move to a smaller house when your children leave home, freeing a portion of your capital gains to be enjoyed while you're still alive. Or you can move when you retire to somewhere with cheaper housing. Or you can remortgage your house, at its new, higher value, to invest in some money-making project in which the returns outstrip the mortgage interest rate – for example, a successful small business.

In all these ways, the value of your house is important. Similar considerations apply with even more force to the value of other fluctuating assets. You don't have to own British Gas shares; so if you do, and their price goes up, you can sell them perfectly cheerfully. These are all good reasons for adding a calculation of your total net worth to the now familiar income and expenditure sums.

How much am I worth?

The starting point for this calculation is the assets and liabilities statement you drew up as part of the last chapter (page 121). That will give you the sum of all your assets, and the liabilities to subtract from them to arrive at your net worth. Take a fresh look at this calculation. Look at each of the elements in turn, and check to see whether you've assessed their value correctly:

The ingredients of wealth

1. **The value of your house.** The real value is what you could get for it if you had to sell it today within a specific period of time, say three months. That might well be 10–15 per cent lower than the price an estate agent might quote you; an agent's estimate is of what you can get if the right buyer comes along, and that may not happen within your time period. Make sure, if you're doing comparison calculations, that you do them realistically. You may firmly believe that your road is much nicer than the one a bit further along; but if the fashion of the moment puts a higher price on the other road, there's nothing you can do about it – and you won't get as much for your house as you think you should. Remember to subtract estate agent fees and other sale costs from the total value of the house.

2. **The value of the endowment policy** you are using to buy the house (if that's the way you're doing it). Ultimately, if you have a 'with profits' policy of some sort, the profits will accumulate enough to make a tidy sum in their own right, over and above the amount you need to pay off the mortgage. The figure you should use for your current wealth calculation, however, is the surrender value, which will be much less than if you hold the policy for its full term. The penalties attached to cashing it in may be so high as to make the exercise unattractive. Cashing the endowment in is often unwise; people who cash in an endowment policy as part of a routine house move are almost certainly losing out.

3. **The value of any other life insurance policies.** If you have any of these, they may have a value; make sure you look at the small print to see what the surrender value is, however. It may well be considerably less than the notional value you've accumulated if you keep the policy going to maturity. (Protection-only term assurance, by the way – the sort of policy you buy simply to pay off in case of death or an accident, with no lump sum or annuity at the end – doesn't have any surrender value.)

4. **The value of your car.** What you're trying to estimate is what you could get for it if you sold it, not its value to you in terms of transportation or sentiment. So don't take the value of a gleaming, as-new specimen; take the price that accurately reflects the value of your car and knock off a bit (up to ten per cent perhaps) to allow for the fact that the calculation is based on sale of the car within a specific period. If your car is a bit exotic – if there aren't many ads for it in either the 'for sale' or 'wanted' sections of the *Automotive Exchange and Mart* – you should knock off another five per cent, because that means it may be hard to find a buyer quickly.

5. **Consumer durables.** For this calculation, take the lower of the depreciated values (as calculated in the last chapter) and what you think you could get for each item by advertising in the local tobacconist's window. As the consumer worksheets suggest, most households have a surprisingly large number of consumer durables today – everything from a camera or video-recorder, to a washing machine – and the total may come to a significant figure. Make sure, though, that you don't include the value of any rented TV sets or video-recorders by mistake.

6. **Investments, savings, etc.** The value you should use for this calculation is market value: how much could you get if you sold your British Gas shares or if you cashed in your National Savings Certificates and your building society account. (Remember that selling shares involves some transaction costs; if you don't know how much they would be, ask a bank or stockbroker for an estimate. Most small transactions – selling £500 worth of British Gas, BP or water company shares, for example – are covered by a broker's

minimum commission, which varies from £20–£50.) Include in this category the value of any gold or (real) silver you may own.

7. **Bank accounts.** Add these up at the end of a period, just before your next salary cheque gets paid in and after all the month's bills have been paid.

8. **Liabilities.** In general, calculate how much you would have to pay if you closed out any loan now; there might well be a pre-payment penalty that needs to be taken into account.

The calculation of how much you're worth that results from all this has its limitations – after all, as your friends will never tire of pointing out, you *do* have to live somewhere. Still, it's the best guide you can get to how much you could realize in a real crisis; and it's the foundation for all the estimates of how your own progress and the fluctuations of the economy affect your family's overall financial health.

The threats to your net worth

There are five possible dangers that threaten your family's overall net worth. These threats affect each household differently, because their impact depends on each family's mix of assets and liabilities. The five threats to your net worth are:

■ Inflation.
■ Adverse interest rate movements.
■ Stock-market slump.
■ Recession.
■ Slumping house prices.

These factors are to some extent inter-related; it's possible to imagine a combination of three or four of them simulta-neously. It's hard, though, to imagine a scenario that includes disaster on all five fronts, because some of them work at cross-purposes to each other, with rises in one danger-element offset, at least in part, by movement in another.

The threat of inflation

Nothing has a more profound impact on asset values than a sharp rise in inflation. Every one per cent rise in the long-term, underlying, rise of inflation has a powerful destructive impact on any assets that are not protected against the damage inflation can cause.

The calculation is a simple one – yet so unpalatable that few people care to make it. Let us assume that all your assets are tied up in some investment paying eight per cent interest. You have £5,000 saved in this way, and you expect inflation over the next five years to run at five per cent a year. You need the interest on that asset to get by on, so you spend it as soon as the cheque arrives. Here is how the value of that asset, and the income stream it generates, looks in terms of constant pounds – the pounds you used to buy the certificates on the day you bought them.

Inflation-adjusted £

Year	Asset Value	Interest
I	5000	400
2	4672	381
3	4535	363
4	4319	346
5	4114	329

As you can see, putting your asset into this form has resulted in an £886, or 18 per cent, decline in its real value over the period, together with a stream of interest payments that dropped in buying power from £400 to £329 during the course of the five years.

Now suppose that inflation, instead of being the five per cent you expected, actually turns out to be six per cent. That one percentage point increase in inflation may not sound like much – but the cumulative impact is not negligible, even over so short a period as five years. Re-calculating the table gives us the following figures:

Inflation-adjusted £

Year	Asset Value	Interest
1	5000	400
2	4717	377
3	4450	356
4	4198	336
5	3960	317

At the end of the period the real value of the asset is now £3960, 21 per cent less than when you first handed it over, and during the time you held it, the value of the yearly nominal £400 in interest declined in real terms to £316.

Over longer periods, and at higher rates, inflation works even more dramatically. Even a one per cent rate of inflation – or a rate of interest that is only one percentage point less than inflation – will destroy a quarter of the value of your capital by the end of 30 years.

It is particularly damaging when combined with the tax system. Because you are taxed on nominal values, not real ones, the combination of a burst of inflation and liability to pay income tax on your interest can be very damaging.

Inflation is an incessant nibbler away at your household assets. Every one percentage point rise in the underlying inflation rate has damaging long-term implications for anyone who has assets which are poorly protected against rising prices.

Stages of inflation

Although every percentage point rise in inflation is, in principle, as bad as another, that's not the way people normally react. In fact, there are several different layers of inflationary damage, and the greatest agony and uncertainty is caused when the rate suddenly moves unexpectedly from one layer to the next.

First stage: 0–4 per cent. During this phase of inflation – for example, the mid-1980s, or post-War Britain until the mid-1960s – people normally ignore inflation for most ordinary purposes. It's nibbling away at your assets, of course, but the damage is sufficiently discreet for you not to expend a lot of energy trying to protect yourself against it. You tend to think of prices as stable, and see the returns you get on your savings or deposit accounts as real ones. The risk in this stage of inflation is a long-term one. In any one year, inflation is low enough not to pose a real danger. But precisely because inflation is not much of a short-term threat, people tend to leave it out of their mental calculations – and over a period of years, stage one inflation can have a damaging impact on the value of savings and other monetary assets.

Second stage: 4–8 per cent. This is the stage Britain went through in the second half of the 1960s and the early part of the 1970s; and again in the late 1980s. Inflation has clearly jumped out of the 'no need to worry' category of the first stage.

It is now a background noise; you expect prices to rise and start to think in 'inflation-plus' terms when it comes to negotiating your pay-rise. But the damage is still not too great: misjudging next year's inflation rate and settling for a pay-rise that's a bit less than inflation will not prove seriously damaging to your family's well-being, because the numbers are not yet big enough to do more short-term damage. Over a longer period of time, however, savings can be rapidly eroded by this level of inflation. At seven per cent inflation, a sum of money halves in value in just over ten years. The biggest risk, however, is probably of a sudden jump out of this range of still-just-about-tolerable inflation to the next one.

Third stage: 8–12 per cent. This is the phase that Britain seemed to be risking entering at the end of 1989, with ten per cent pay-rises starting to look dangerously like the norm. In this range, it's easy to make a mistake and suffer immediate and painful consequences.

Settling for too low a pay-rise – or having no choice in accepting it because the financial condition of your firm is so poor – can very rapidly lower your family's standard of living. Suppose you settle for a seven per cent pay-rise for a year in which inflation ends up rising to 11 per cent by the closing months. By the last month of the year, you'll be getting four per cent less in real terms than you earned 12 months before – a very sharp reduction in living standards. To put that in concrete terms, if you were earning £20,000 before the pay-rise, at the end of the year in which you got it you'd be £15-a-week worse off, in pre-tax income, than before.

Assets are equally vulnerable: and again, the damage can be rapid, taking effect before you notice. Leaving money in a savings account earning six per cent when inflation is running at nine per cent will soon start to shrivel the true value of your savings. If the interest you're receiving is taxed at 40 per cent, the impact is even greater: at the end of the year, you're 3.1 per cent worse off than at the beginning of the year.

Fourth stage: 12 per cent plus. Once inflation reaches this level, it's so all-pervasive that every family financial decision is dominated by it. There's a general flight out of assets denominated in treacherous, unstable money, and towards real assets: land, gold, diamonds, vintage cars, eighteenth-century silver, first editions, and so on. We haven't seen this level of inflation since 1979–80; with luck we won't see it again. But if it looks as though inflation is headed in this direction, batten down the hatches.

Adverse interest rate movements

As the tabloids might put it: one family's Interest Rate Misery is another family's Savings Bonanza. If you're a net debtor (and your interest payments move up and down in line with the overall level of interest rates) a rise in rates is very bad news. If you're a net creditor, receiving interest payments tied to the day-to-day or month-to-month level of interest rates, a rise in rates is extremely good news. In the past, the difference between the two categories used to be largely one of age. Younger people borrowed money; older people, their mortgages being repaid, had a surplus of savings over borrowings. A rise in interest rates was a blow for the younger generation against the older; a drop in interest rates made it better to be young than old.

That's changed a bit, partly because everybody is borrowing more, partly because the surge in house prices in the late 1980s was so rapid and so large. The division has now shifted from a straightforward old/young one to a split that reflects the date at which you bought your house. Mid-80s house buyers are much less vulnerable to a rise in interest rates than those who bought at the top of the market a few years later. Of course, there's still a link with age: the very youngest families don't feature in the low-mortgage group at all, because they weren't around to acquire one. But among middle-aged and older people, it is harder to work out whether they're gainers or losers from interest rate movements just by counting the grey hairs.

Anyway, financial sociology aside, how great is the threat of an adverse interest rate movement? Bear in mind this rule of thumb:

■ In the short run (a year or so) nominal interest rate changes are what matter.

■ In the longer term (12 months plus) it's *real*
interest rate changes that count.

The implication is obvious if you think of how a big change in
interest rates hits. Let's suppose interest rates are eight per cent
and inflation is around six per cent. If interest rates rise, in a
matter of months, from eight to ten per cent, people who pay
and receive interest get the full effect of all two percentage
points. Monthly mortgage payments go up by a quarter; the
amount of money a building society pays you each month on
your nest-egg goes up by the same proportion.

As time passes, though, the real impact of that rise depends
crucially on what's happened to the rate of inflation. If the
inflation rate is still six per cent, then the two percentage point
rise in interest rates is a *real* one. Homebuyers are stuck with
paying those higher interest payments out of pay packets that
are going up in line with an increased rate of inflation – one
that doesn't match the sharp increase in interest rates.
Similarly, those with nest-eggs have got a nice extra payment
which isn't being eaten away by inflation any faster than it was
before.

If the rise in interest rates isn't a rise in *real* interest rates, but
only in *nominal* ones, however, the picture is quite different.
The impact of higher interest rates is sooner or later
neutralized by a higher rate of inflation. Since wages usually
rise more or less in line with inflation, those higher mortgage
payments must come out of pay packets that are growing more
rapidly than before. That's still painful, but the sting is less.
Similarly, the bonus to savers is soon eroded by the rise in the
price of the things the higher interest payments can buy.

An adverse change in real interest rates – moving higher if
you're a net debtor, lower if you're a net creditor – is
potentially a damaging threat to your family's wealth.

The threat of a recession

Since a recession normally dampens down inflation, one of its effects is beneficial for people who own monetary assets. Those people, however, who have built themselves anti-inflation hedges (such as a heavy reliance on an expensive house, or other 'real assets' from gold to antiques) may find that a recession hits their overall net worth. This is partly because the dampening effect of a recession on inflation undermines the attractiveness of assets bought in the expectation of rapidly rising prices. It is partly also because it may be harder to sell such assets – which are basically luxuries rather than essentials – if a recession makes everybody worse off.

The threat of a stock-market slump

This can be a special case of the threat of a recession. The stock market usually falls ahead of a recession, as investors anticipate the coming slide in company profits. Sometimes, however, a stock-market slide isn't limited to an up-coming recession – either because investors' guesses about the outlook are wrong, or because they're anticipating a squeeze on corporate profits as a result of other factors (for example, a Labour Party victory at a general election).

A stock-market slump affects those people who own shares – a much wider slice of the population than ten years ago. Even though many families own shares, however, most of the new investors hold only one or two stocks, usually privatization issues. As a proportion of most people's wealth, stocks and shares are far less important than houses. None the less, though families own few shares directly, they may own them indirectly through unit trust-linked insurance policies, for instance.

A slumping stock market, by reducing the values of those assets, has an indirect effect on family wealth. It also makes it more expensive for companies to meet their pension obligations, reducing the chances of any largesse (for example, inflation-linked upgrading of pension payments) over and above the minimum. In these indirect ways, a weak stock market can feed through into the wealth of every family – even those that wouldn't recognize a share certificate if it bit them in the ankles.

The threat of falling house prices

For most people this is the biggest threat of all to family wealth. That is partly because household ownership is such an important proportion of family wealth – so even small swings in the value of a house have an important impact on the wealth of the family that owns it. It is also because of the feature of house purchase that makes it such an attractive investment.

The power of gearing. Gearing – or as the Americans say, leverage – is simply investing with borrowed money. It is an enormously powerful way of amplifying the effect of any investment – amplifying it either for good or ill. That's why governments, regulators or lending institutions typically limit the amount of gearing anyone can undertake. For ordinary people, few highly-geared investments are possible – except for houses.

Why is gearing important? Take an example. Suppose you have inherited £50,000, and plan to buy a house with it. You're scared of borrowing, so you don't take out a mortgage. You buy a £50,000-house entirely with cash. In five years, the value of the house doubles. In nominal terms (without allowing for inflation) your money has doubled: a 100 per cent return. Not bad; quite a lot better than you'd have got from most forms of saving.

Suppose, however, that you don't happen to start off with £50,000; you have £5,000 instead. Your family income is high enough to get you a £45,000 mortgage, however, so you can still buy the house. In five years, the value of the house doubles. Your asset is once again worth £100,000 – but this time, you've achieved that return on an initial stake of £5,000, not £50,000. The return is not 100 per cent, but 1,900 per cent.

(You may think I've made a mistake in this calculation by leaving out the interest you have to pay on a mortgage. Though I have to pay a mortgage in the second case, however, I have to give up the use of my £50,000 in the first case: there is an 'opportunity cost' to you of tying up the money in bricks and mortar instead of lending it out and earning interest. So either way, there is an interest factor involved – forgone or actually paid – and that doesn't affect the basic calculation.)

Gearing is an enormously powerful way of amplifying the impact of an investment, so it's not surprising that many of the great post-War fortunes are built around using other people's money in this way.

But gearing works both ways: it can be enormously destructive as well as enormously rewarding – which is why its use is so strictly rationed.

Take the same examples as before, and make only one change: a 20 per cent drop in the price of the house. At the end of five years, the house is worth only £40,000. In the first case, the family that poured its inheritance into the house is hurt: its windfall is now worth 20 per cent less than when it started. But it still has a house worth £40,000, so the picture is not *too* gloomy. Compare that with the paper position of the second family. It invested £5,000 in the house, and borrowed £45,000. But the house is now worth only £40,000 – so instead of losing only 20 per cent of its initial investment, the family has lost 200 per cent of it. If the house had to be sold, therefore, the family would have no deposit, no house – and it would *still* owe £5,000 to the bank on an asset that no longer exists.

This has almost never happened since the great shift towards a property-owning democracy got under way after the Second World War. Prices have risen steadily; and a heavily-geared bet on a one-way price escalator is about the closest thing imaginable to finding money in the street. Even when the housing market was soft – in the mid-1970s, for example – inflation was so high that house prices merely marked time for a bit, and didn't fall in absolute terms. The one-way escalator juddered, paused, but didn't go into reverse.

Until now.

The drop in house prices, particularly marked in London, since the autumn of 1988, has produced for some people exactly the effects of the heavily-geared price decline described above. What seemed, for nearly half a century, merely a hypothetical possibility has turned into fact. On paper, for some people, the gearing of the mortgage machine has worked the other way. It has gobbled up the value of 'equity' (the householder's stake in the house – in this case, the original cash deposit). And it has left the loans underwater, as bankers say – that is, secured against property that is now worth less than the value of the loans.

So far, however, these cases are few. Banks and building societies will typically lend 90 per cent of the value of a house, so a borrower's house would have to drop in price by ten per cent to wipe out all the equity; by more to put the loan underwater. By the end of 1989, house prices might have dropped by at least that much in London from their peak of 18 months before, but nobody really wanted to find out. The housing market had dried up, with houseowners unwilling to turn their paper losses into real ones, and building societies and banks showing no inclination to push them into making such an unpleasant discovery – even when rising interest rates had led purchasers to drop behind on their mortgage payments.

You can see, though, why highly-geared house purchase has been the engine for wealth creation for so many years – and why, if things really go wrong, it can turn into a machine for destroying family wealth instead.

What will happen to house prices?

Your guess is as good as mine: the hardest sort of guess about any market is the attempt to work out whether you've just reached a temporary breathing place, or whether some fundamental changes have taken place that will reverse a trend that seemed set in concrete. There are arguments on both sides:

The 'breathing space' theory. The best guide to house prices, over many years, has been the level of incomes. When the ratio of house prices to incomes gets too high, the house price escalator slows or stops; it may even lead to a drop in prices in real terms. We've had such drops before, but they've always been concealed by high inflation. Now, inflation is obvious, so the drop in real prices is a drop in nominal prices as well. But that's no big deal. In time, prices will start upwards again once the house price/wage level is back in line. They will do so because the long-run trend is unwavering, based on three factors:

- The attraction of house purchase as an investment (gearing, mortgage interest income tax relief, exemption from capital gains tax when you sell the house)
- The insatiable demand for more housing space as families splinter and not-in-my-backyard limits on new building create an even greater shortage of housing land
- Everyone expects house prices always to go up, so they will

The 'doomster' theory. In Germany, until the influx of East European refugees, house prices had fallen not just in real terms but in nominal ones for much of the past decade. This fact, which most British homeowners (including me) find hard to accept, is none the less true. It means that another developed country not that dissimilar to Britain has had an entirely different house price experience, and suggests that there is nothing pre-ordained about the UK's one-way escalator. Apart from this general point, there are a number of other reasons for thinking that the forces that have propelled the house price boom may be waning:

- There's a growing consensus among people who influence economic policy that the housing market weakens the British economy, and makes it far harder to control. The recession that's on the horizon is the hangover from a boom that got out of hand, partly because house prices boomed so recklessly in the late 1980s. Mrs Thatcher's Government is unlikely to dismantle the artificial attractions of house purchase; the next one, of whatever political colour, might start to do so
- The ageing population means that fewer and fewer people are joining the bottom of the house-purchase ladder – and in the absence of pressure from below, house prices will rise much more slowly. At the top of the ladder, middle-aged baby boomers will be freeing up space as they move to smaller accommodation once their children leave home; and once their home-owning parents die, they'll be selling off the property they inherited
- Everyone expects house prices always to go up, so they're sure to fall

Weighing up the risks to your family

The risks of those five threats will vary from family to family, from household to household. And, of course, some of the dangers are more likely to come true than others. So a full risk-assessment will weigh up:

- How likely each risk is, on a Risk Rating of 1 to 5
- How exposed your family is to each one, on an Exposure Rating of 1 to 5
- How damaging an adverse outcome could be, on a Damage Rating of 1 to 5.

To take a simple example, if you own no shares, then a stock-market slump has no direct impact on you; and if you're still some way from retirement, the indirect threat of a stock-market slump to pension trustees' generosity is unlikely to concern you much. Risk Rating may be 3, but Exposure Rating only 1. There'll be many more stock-market ups and downs before you start to draw your pension.

To take another example, you may not think a house-price slump is very likely – Risk Rating 2; Damage Rating 2 – but if your principal asset is the equity in your house, your finances are constantly exposed to it: Exposure Rating 5. Again, though, the significance of that exposure depends on the circumstances: if you don't need to move and can continue to meet your mortgage payments, even an underwater house loan is not too damaging (as long as you expect house prices to recover in the long run). Damage Rating here is 2. However, if you were planning to sell the house and move to something smaller, using the profits to allow you to retire early, any threat to the value of the equity in your house is much more harmful: Damage Rating 4.

Before you take steps to protect yourself against these wealth-destroying forces, you need to make a systematic attempt to classify the risks. Follow this checklist:

Inflation. The history of Britain – and the world, come to that – since the First World War proves that this is the likeliest risk of all, with a Risk Rating between 3 and 5, depending on how pessimistic you are. Even when inflation is held down, the levels to which it is restrained – say four per cent a year – are still enough to halve the value of your money in 20 years, well within your long-term planning horizon if you have small children, a mortgage or hopes of a pension. And unless British economic policy escapes from the hands of British politicians (perhaps, through membership of an expanded European Monetary System, into the hands of German central bankers) there is every likelihood that inflation will burst out again and again, leaping from the first stage of inflation (see page 144) to the second and third stages. Never again, we pray, will it reach the fourth, sky's the limit, stage – though even that isn't certain.

If the likelihood is high, how exposed are you to inflation? In particular:

- How likely is it that your pay-rises will keep up with rising prices (not just the rises reflected in the national Retail Prices Index, but the prices of the bundle of goods and services you buy, in the place where you live)? Typical Exposure Rating here will be 1 or 2, rising to 3 or 4 if you happen to have a poor bargaining position or an impoverished employer.

- Are you owed, or do you receive, any fixed sums of money? If so, you're exposed, because inflation will rapidly erode their value. The Exposure Rating varies with the amount concerned. Note that pensions or insurance products in which the ultimate payment is fixed in money terms (rather than as a proportion of your final salary) are vulnerable, too. And where your pension is calculated as the return on the money you (and perhaps your employer) are investing, how confident are you that the likely returns will outstrip inflation?

- Do you have any financial assets on which the rewards would be negative if inflation rose a couple more percentage points? If you have any fixed-interest assets, or if you keep large sums of money in no- or low-interest current or deposit accounts, you could be at risk on this score. Again, if these sums are a significant proportion of your total worth, the Exposure Rating could be 4 or 5; lower if the sums are smaller.

How dangerous is this exposure? You'll obviously have to judge that for yourself – but inflation, through the magic of compound interest, is particularly damaging over long periods of time. So if your exposure is of the sort where the final impact of inflation can't be seen for many years (as in some types of savings vehicles) the long-term impact of continued stage-two or -three inflation is great. Damage Rating here is 3 or 4.

Adverse interest rate movements. The likelihood that, at some time in the near future, you'll be affected by adverse interest rate movements is high: Risk Rating at least 3, probably 4 or 5. And that holds good whether you benefit (as a net saver) from higher interest rates or whether you suffer, as a net borrower, from them. The reason is that interest rates seem set for continued sharp movements. For much of the nineteenth century, interest rates were unchanged – you got about three per cent on a solid investment, and that was that. Even as recently as the 1950s, interest rates went unchanged for years. Now, they move like a roller coaster.

In the 1990s, volatility is here to stay. But that means that though the short-term impact of *nominal* interest rates may be high, their longer-term impact is less damaging – simply because before too long they'll have reversed course.

More worrying, probably, is the impact of *real* interest rates. There seems to have been a shift towards permanently higher real interest rates in the early 1980s. A shift back, to lower (or even negative) real interest rates, would profoundly alter the relative attractions of saving and borrowing.

Because interest rates have now been so volatile for so long, both your liabilities and your monetary assets are likely to be floating-rate ones, in which the interest you pay or receive goes up and down with the general level of rates.

That is more effective for changes in nominal interest rates than for real ones. In fact, about the only assets you can purchase that give you a guaranteed *real* rate of interest are index-linked gilts and National Savings Certificates, both issued by the Government.

None the less, most people's interest rate exposure is tied to their biggest single liability, their mortgage. The risk is twofold. In the short run, a sharp rise in interest rates might outstrip your ability to finance the mortgage out of income. In the longer term, a rise in real interest rates will reduce the attractiveness of the house as an investment (especially if house prices are flat or falling), and raise the burden of carrying the loan despite any pay-rises you may receive in the meantime.

So, how exposed are you to interest rate fluctuations?

- What proportion of after-tax household income goes on servicing debt (including your mortgage)? If the ratio is a high one – over a third, say, – your Exposure Rating is up in the 4 to 5 range. If it's lower, say under 15 per cent, the Exposure Rating drops away to 1 or 2.

- How big an impact would a further one per cent rise in interest rates have on your after-tax income? This is another way of asking the same question. If a one per cent rise in interest rates gobbles up more than 1–2 per cent of your after-tax income, your Exposure Rating is close to 4. If the figure is three per cent or more, the Exposure Rating is 5.

- What proportion of your income depends on floating-rate interest payments? This is for people who derive income from investments that pay interest, such as pensioners who have invested past savings in floating-rate accounts. If more than 30 per cent of your income depends on the exact level of floating interest rates, you could be exposed to a nasty shock when rates go down – especially if they move sharply back towards Continental levels, say a drop of five percentage points. Exposure Rating here is 4 or 5. Lower exposure obviously produces a lower Rating.

■ How would a one per cent drop in interest rates affect your household income? This is a way of putting a hard-cash figure on your answer to the last question. If a one per cent drop in interest rates produces, say, a seven to eight per cent drop in your income, you should award yourself an Exposure Rating of 4 or more. A smaller impact would produce a lower Rating.

How dangerous is this exposure? Interest rates usually move up or down in discrete steps, so the short-term damage of any individual move is low. None the less, abrupt moves in interest rates are possible over quite short periods, as in 1988–89. For most people, the potential damage is probably not too high – a Damage Rating of 2 at most. For those people whose financial calculations only really work on the basis of unchanged interest rates, however, the Danger Rating is higher, 3 or 4 or more.

Recession. The Risk Rating here is at least 3. But the impact of recession, if one comes, is not so much on people's wealth as on their income. So doing a risk-estimate on the wealth side of the issue may seem a bit irrelevant. And unless you've taken the fear of inflation so completely to heart that your pattern of debts and assets is completely skewed towards fighting it, the Exposure Rating, which measures how exposed your assets are to the risk of a recession, will be low, around 1 or 2.

Two exceptions, however:

■ If the family wealth is tied up in a small business that could go bust if recession strikes, your Exposure Rating to this threat is 3 or 4 or more.
■ If you carry on fighting inflation too doggedly *after* it becomes clear that a shift in government policy towards eliminating it is so complete and

comprehensive that the financial markets are completely convinced. In this case, you'd have an Exposure Rating of 3 or 4.

In the second set of circumstances, a pattern of assets and liabilities that was very sensible when you were expecting continued high inflation may be inappropriate, as some people found in the early 1980s. How such a government shift of policy is likely to be you must judge for yourself; in general, it's fair to say that for most people the threat of inflation continuing is far more serious than the threat that it will come to an abrupt end.

Unless you fall into one or other of these two categories, the potential damage to your wealth from a recession is slight: Damage Rating 1 or so. If you are covered by the two special cases, however, the damage could be considerable: Damage Rating 3 at least.

Stock-market slump. Shares, as the stock-market regulators like to remind us, can go down as well as up. The threat of a slide in equity values – in real, if not in nominal terms – is always present. How exposed you are to such a development depends on the proportion of your family's wealth that's in shares: for most people, not a lot directly, but rather more perhaps through such saving mechanisms as unit-linked life insurance policies.

Although the absolute amount of exposure may not be high, the consequences of a stock-market slump could be very damaging. If you need money in a hurry, you may have no choice but to liquidate your shares at very unfavourable prices. Or your unit-linked policy may mature in a stock-market trough, reducing the gains you'd expected.

It would not be surprising if most people display rather an uneven pattern of ratings on this issue – a Risk Rating of 4 or 5 (because at some point the stock market *will* go down); an

Exposure Rating of only 1 or 2, even allowing for indirect interests in the stock market; but a Damage Rating of 3 or 4, because a stock-market slump could do severe damage to that portion of your wealth (or expectations) that is exposed to it.

House prices. The risk of a real house-price collapse is probably not high, though you should make your own assessment (see box, page 152). Your exposure, however, is likely to be very high indeed: a definite 5, unless you're living in rented accommodation. Assess the damage it would cause by how your house figures in your financial plans, and how appropriate it is for your medium-term plans. Award a higher Damage Rating if cashing in your house equity is an important part of your near-term planning; or if job changes or family pressures are likely to force you to move with little control over timing.

How to protect yourself

The five risks to your family's financial well-being – inflation, interest rate changes, a stock-market slump, recession or falling houses prices – all demand a basic approach to defending yourself. This can be summed up in three words:

Think. Control. Diversify.

Thinking is what you've been doing so far in this chapter. It means taking a rational approach to assessing the risks you face, on concentrating on protecting yourself against those that pose the biggest threat.

If you multiply the three rating figures in each category together, you'll get a risk-profile for your own family. There's no really scientific way of assigning ratings, so the numbers you come up with can't really be compared with some notional 'average' or 'ideal' scale. I'd guess that for most people, the likely scale will range from 6 or so to around 60. That isn't the point, however. The ratings are useful because they give you a

Health Warning

■ This book, I'm afraid, is not a comprehensive personal finance guide. There are lots of those already available, and you will almost certainly find one that suits you in your local bookshop.

What this book tries to do is to help you relate the economic outlook to your own circumstances, as you start to build an action plan for survival and prosperity. Part of that action plan will inevitably involve further research, and perhaps the services of a professional financial adviser.

I'm therefore very aware, as I write this chapter, how many investment wrinkles I'm smoothing over, how many interesting opportunities for earning a good return aren't mentioned. If you feel the particular scheme, wheeze or investment plan you've discovered is better than the few plain-vanilla ones mentioned here, I can only wish you every success.

Remember, though, that anyone reading this chapter in hope of finding the best money-market fund or the most competitive building society account is missing the point: the weekend financial pages or the *Investors Chronicle* will do the job in a far more up-to-date fashion.

The aim here is to sound an alert over the threats to your wealth and financial well-being; and to signal the directions in which protection and prosperity can be sought.

list of priorities: start by tackling the risks with the highest scores. You may never get around to the lower ones – it's impossible to live a risk-free life anyway. Remember, though, to keep the ratings up to date, as your exposure to these risks varies (partly in response to the steps you'll be undertaking) and your expectations about the economy change: what looked like a small risk – inflation in 1986, for example – can suddenly turn into a big one, and vice versa.

Think also about tax. Taxation on the income from savings is far less onerous than it was; but it's still capable of interaction with inflation (or any of the other threats to wealth) to chisel away the difference between a positive rate of return and a shrinking of your original capital. Tax strategy for investors fills many books, but some basic general principles are:

- Tax-break saving is usually far more effective than saving that has to carry the full burden of income tax both on the money you put in and the returns you get. So make the most of the few opportunities you get to build up assets out of untaxed income (the first tax-deductible part of your mortgage, and your pension plan). And seek out opportunities, such as Personal Equity Plans, that let you avoid passing income and capital gains tax on the assets you accumulate.
- The transformation of the pension rules (see Step 7) has greatly widened the opportunities to invest through tax-advantaged pension vehicles.
- The change to independent taxation of husbands and wives, which started in April 1990, will alter the investment opportunities open to many families. A wife's 'unearned' (ie, investment) income will no longer be taxed at the rate her husband pays on his top slice of income. And if one spouse works and the other doesn't, they will benefit from holding their savings in the non-working partner's name in an account which pays interest gross, rather than tax-deducted.
- And remember the other tax: capital gains tax, which is likely to make a return as an inconvenience if inflation continues to create 'paper' increases in value on which capital gains tax could be charged. Home sales are free of capital gains tax; so are profits on gilts. The rate you pay is the same as the top slice of your income tax. But

you're allowed to realize a healthy slice of capital gains a year tax free.

Controlling your exposure and the damage it can cause is the key to coping with financial risks. Try not to drift into a high exposure to something that has a high Risk or Damage Rating without thinking what you're doing. When an insurance salesman offers you a particular policy or product, for example, try to assess two things:

- How does this product, on its own, stand up on the Risk/Exposure/Damage Ratings?
- Just as important, how does it affect your overall risk-profile? Does it add to your exposure to a risk with a high probability and worrying potential for damage? Or does it offset it?

Similar criteria should be applied to any decision that will have an important effect on the pattern of the family's assets and liabilities.

Diversifying means actively attempting to spread out your risks and limiting your exposure to the ones with the highest probability and the greatest potential for damage.

Diversifying to counter the five threats

1. **Inflation.** Hold as little cash as possible in current accounts and low-yielding deposit accounts. (In early 1990, with the inflation rate running at eight per cent or so, a building society ordinary share account yielded an after-tax interest rate of only just over five per cent to a taxpayer in the 40 per cent bracket – that is, anyone with a taxable income of over £20,700. That money was depreciating at an annual rate of roughly three per cent – enough to halve it in value in just

under 23 years. A customer with a bank deposit account was one percentage point worse off still.)

Use any surplus cash to reduce credit-card or other borrowings, or try to collect it together to qualify for the higher rates available to larger depositors in banks or building societies. The same building society providing an after-tax return of just over five per cent on ordinary share accounts was providing the same taxpayer with over seven per cent on an instant-access account with more than £2,000 in it.

And look for other means of diversifying your nest-egg to protect it against inflation. Someone in the same tax bracket could have obtained over nine per cent after tax from a money market account or a high-interest bank or building society account. They could have obtained the same after-tax return from index-linked government securities (index-linked gilts) – though they would have had to accept the risk that the value of the capital they had invested might fluctuate over time. Alternatively, if they were prepared to lock up the money in index-linked National Savings Certificates for five years, they could have received a tax-free rate of return, after inflation, of over four per cent.

For long-run saving, however, it is desirable to balance these safe fixed-interest investments with a holding (perhaps through a unit trust) of shares. These do not promise to match, in dividends, the returns available in fixed-interest stocks; but they hold out the possibility of long-term capital growth in the value of the shares as the companies in which they reflect an ownership position prosper.

2. **Interest rate changes.** The days when you could easily protect yourself against likely interest rate changes by borrowing at a fixed rate are long gone. Inflation made that too much of a one-way bet at the lender's expense. (If interest rates fell, you could always take out a replacement loan at a lower rate. If they rose, you smiled all the way to the bank.) Some fixed-rate mortgages are available, but they come surrounded with enough in the way of up-front fees or prepayment penalties to prevent their use as a one-way bet. None the less, if you are taking out a new mortgage, there are a number of offerings available that can limit the cash flow shock of a rise in interest rates by providing a short-term

ceiling on payments. It's worth shopping around; most people don't.

If you're a creditor, rather than a debtor, you can protect yourself against a sharp drop in interest rates by lending the money at a fixed rate, for example, through National Savings Certificates, an insurance company guaranteed income bond or a building society fixed-interest account (also often called a bond). If you thought interest rates were in danger of dropping sharply, the fixed, relatively high, rate offered might hold out the prospect of a significant real after-tax return. You would have to set against that possibility, however, the risk that inflation and interest rates roared ahead making higher interest rates available elsewhere.

3. **A stock-market slump.** You can diversify to offset the risks of the UK stock market by investing in foreign unit trusts; you can build a measure of protection against the risks of all types of shares by ensuring that you hold other types of securities, such as gilts.

4. **Recession.** Diversifying your assets to hedge against the impact of a recession means: making sure you don't have all your family assets in a business which could go bust in a recession; making sure you've got some means of raising cash in a hurry, and that your assets aren't all illiquid or restricted ones; and making sure that you haven't invested so heavily in traditional 'inflation hedges', such as gold, that you're badly affected by the drop in the price of such items that tends to accompany a recession.

If you can carry out the Think–Control–Diversify cycle often enough – once every couple of years or so – you should find that your Risk Ratings gradually drop, or at least that you have a better idea what your risks are, and where the vulnerabilities lie.

Taking advantage of the bad times
Prospering in a recession or during an inflationary period isn't all a question of trying to hold on to what you've got. With the proper combination of planning and opportunism, you can

make the most of a time of flux and uncertainty. For at such moments do bargains occur.

The keys to taking advantage of the bad times are: to be prepared (with money you can quickly use to snap up a bargain either in your possession or lined up beforehand); and to watch out for long-term value that is underpriced because of the circumstances of the moment. Some possible examples follow:

Seven ways to turn a crisis into an opportunity

1. **Undervalued shares.** When times are bad, share prices fall, taking the good down along with the bad. That can be a real opportunity to acquire assets at a bargain price. But sorting out the good from the bad is no easier in a slump than in a boom. In some ways it can be harder, because the amount of 'noise' in the background is greater and more menacing: announcements of factory closures, bankruptcies, grim macroeconomic facts, all make it harder to focus on the true value of the company you're interested in. Some general rules:
   - *Be prepared to do some work on this.* Put some time into researching possible share purchases by getting information from the company and from Companies House, and visiting a business library to read up on the firm, its industry, markets and competitors
   - *Choose companies you know something about.* Not your own (that would be putting too many eggs in one basket) but ones you've been able to observe closely, as customers, suppliers or neighbours. A bit of first-hand knowledge is your best advantage over the highly-paid City investment managers. They've got instant access to all the public information; but it's much harder for them to know the service the sales force gives or the smile on the face of the day-shift once orders are starting to flow again
   - *Look for a company with undervalued assets.* That way, even if the management can't handle the recession, there'll still be enough value for you to do well out of the firm in a forced sale or breakup. Assets to watch out for include land, of course, and some other tangibles – but they also include valuable brand names, a powerful distribution system and patent rights

■ *Diversify.* The chances are you won't have a great deal of money to invest, and you'll want to try to concentrate this for maximum effect. None the less, resist the temptation to make a single large bet. Particularly when times are hard, that can prove very dangerous. No matter how thoroughly you've done your homework, there will always be some pitfall you've failed to foresee. That's when you'll be grateful you divided your nest-egg between a couple of rival investments

■ *Remember that 'bottom-fishing' is a risky business.* Don't invest in the assumption that the share price has reached the bottom, and that things can only get better. They can *always* get worse; and even if you've correctly identified the bottom, the company may bump along it for quite some time. Focus your investment on the inherent value in the company. That way, even if the price subsequently drops further, you won't be too dispirited: you still get a bargain; it's just that it wasn't quite as good value as it might have been

2. **Part-completed projects.** When bad times strike, people who started on a project without proper capital frequently run out of money and work comes to a halt. That's a good time to get a bargain: because the project is only part-completed, it's not very attractive to a purchaser. This principle applies to projects as big as Brighton Marina (which Brent Walker bought for a song in a part-completed state and turned into an extremely valuable asset) or as small as the house a few doors along where the developer ran out of money half-way through turning it into flats. The pay-offs are potentially great – but the risks are great, too. Some ways of guarding against them:

■ *Make sure you know what you're doing.* A project is only a bargain if you can successfully bring it to fruition. Do you have the skill to do that? Can you find a partner who does?

■ *Make sure you've got enough capital to complete.* Don't find yourself in the same mess as the person you take over from: only go into such a venture if you have the wherewithal to see it through even on the most pessimistic assumptions

■ *Work back from a realistic exit.* Just because something *seems* cheap, don't assume automatically that it's a bargain – even if you're getting it for less than the money that's been sunk into it already. Instead, work backwards from the price you could get for it once everything is complete and working properly. And allow for the fact that you'll have to invest *now* in return for a pay-off some time in the *future* . A good small business guide will tell you how to do the discounted cash-flow analysis that will allow you to compare the future return with today's investment on a realistic basis

3. **Management buyouts.** As companies retrench in a recession, they often search for ways to sell unwanted subsidiaries or divisions as a going concern. That avoids redundancy costs – and it lets the parent company avoid the bad publicity of closing something down and the managerial time that would otherwise have to go into negotiating with trade unions and local politicians over the details of the closure. The easiest and quickest sale can often be to the unit's own managers, who know most about the business and are able to assess its value quickly. The good news is that these management buyouts are now a routine transaction, and a whole host of lenders and advisers have sprung up to help the managers turn themselves into owners. The bad news is that, precisely because they are so common, their value is much more clearly understood – and the astonishing bargains to be had in the early days have now largely disappeared. None the less, in a recession the parent company's urge to sell quickly will return, and the days of bargains may come back with it. There are good, free, guides to organizing a management buyout to be obtained from lenders, like 3i, and the units that the big banks have set up to specialize in this area. Remember a few rules of thumb:
   ■ *Don't overpay.* Stand back and try to look at the business dispassionately. What are its strengths and weaknesses? Where do its products stand on the Instant Strategy diagram (page 81). Remember that, for the first time, you'll be dealing with your own money – so be extremely chary about any suggestion from your boss that an extra £500,000 on the buyout price would make everything much easier

- *Get enough working capital.* Make sure that the financial structure of the buyout allows you to survive that first very difficult year. You'll have lots of problems to deal with: lack of working capital shouldn't be one of them. This rule of thumb goes along with the first one. Because the lenders will probably have a very clear idea of how much they're prepared to lend on the business, any extra money that goes into the buyout price probably comes straight out of working capital. And that can prove fatal
- *Plan slowly, move quickly.* Start thinking about a possible management buyout long before one becomes plausible. Get information, make tentative contact with lenders, sketch out a business plan. Then, once it seems a buyout is on the cards, move very quickly to head off possible sales to outsiders or liquidation. Speed at this stage is much easier if you're not starting from scratch
- *Make sure your family's behind you.* A buyout places enormous stress on all concerned. It's important that your family feels comfortable with what you're planning to do, and understands the demands it will place on everyone. If you find your spouse is unhappy with the likely burdens involved, you should think twice about the proposal. Money isn't everything; sometimes family happiness comes first
- *Teamwork is essential.* The new management team will have to work much more closely together, partly because you'll no longer have head office to rely on. So make sure that the team contains all the strengths you need, and that its members are happy with one another. You may need to bring in specialist skills from outside (especially in finance, which might often have been handled at head office up till now). And you may need to be ruthless with some of your senior colleagues. The need for teamwork extends right through the new company, however. Since there'll almost certainly be something wrong with the company when you buy it – otherwise, why are they selling? – you'll need to make rapid improvements. Motivating the work force is the key to a successful turnaround, so don't be greedy: share the ownership of the company, and the potential rewards, as widely as possible
- *Act quickly once the deal is done.* People will be expecting

change, and though they may not relish it, they will accept it if it comes quickly. After a few months, however, if things go on as they always used to, people will come to expect no change – and so resent it when it comes. So do as much as possible as quickly as possible: change the organization and work patterns, axe the weak bits of the product line, change the corporate identity, and so on. All these things will take months of argument with entrenched interests unless you're able to take advantage of the window of change open after the deal. Combine these changes with an immediate blitz on costs (to symbolize the new, tight-fisted era) and a few symbolic investments in the future, such as repainting the canteen (to symbolize the visionary side of the new era)

■ *Cash is king.* As a subsidiary, you have probably been insulated from the obsession with cash that dominates the lives of independent small businesses. Your measure of success has probably been profits or return on sales. Now you must focus on cash, particularly in a recession. Recast all your monthly reporting to put the emphasis on cash. Insist that any proposal that comes to you is cast in terms of its cash implications. Cut inventories to the bone, and then cut again. And make everyone who has any dealings with customers realize that the prompt, polite, extraction of cash is an essential part of everyone's job

4. **Departmental spin-offs.** If management buyouts were the trend of the 1980s, departmental spin-offs could be the trend of the 1990s. In fact, the trend is so new that it hasn't got a proper name yet: I've made up my own. These spin-offs take place when a company decides that it doesn't need to perform a certain internal function itself – the mailroom, the in-house print shop – but would be better off subcontracting it. Sometimes it simply hands over the task to an outside supplier. But there's no reason why the outside supplier couldn't be the person who's running the operation already. If that's you, you become a small business owner overnight, often without having to pay for the privilege. Some points to bear in mind:

■ *Get the pricing right.* The single biggest issue for your new business in its first year is the price it charges to its new giant customer. It's essential to agree a realistic price, one that both sides feel happy with. You'll probably, as an internal department, be charging a price to customers already. Don't assume for a moment that this is the price you should be charging once you're independent. Start with a clean sheet of paper, and try to assess all the costs that go into providing the service. If the end result is higher than the internally-charged price, that merely means the internal price isn't a realistic one, and you'll have to convince your new customer that it's been incurring big hidden costs that will now vanish. Remember also to construct a pricing formula that charges the customer for each incremental service supplied – otherwise you'll find yourself inundated with requests for services that cost the customer nothing, yet place a heavy burden on you. In the old days, if that happened, you could just say 'Sorry, can't do it this week'. In the new era that won't be tenable

■ *Diversify your customers.* As long as you only have one customer, it will always be able to drive a hard bargain – with the advantage of knowing pretty accurately what your costs are. So diversify quickly, by offering the same service to others. Try to go for a few other big customers, rather than lots of small ones; to start with, at least, you're sure to underestimate the costs involved in serving small customers

■ *Motivate the work force.* The key to your success will be in getting the work force to be more productive than in the days when they were just a cost centre. Possible steps include: sharing out ownership; paying more, but expecting a *lot* more in terms of effort and commitment; changing pay structure completely on to a performance-related basis, and so on

■ *Plan for the future.* In a true management buyout, there's usually a clear objective: going public in three to five years. In a departmental spin-off, the objectives are not so clear. It's easy to think in terms of preserving the *status quo*, being your own boss and maybe making a bit more money. Try to set out a more ambitious plan for the future: a set of business objectives (for example, five customers, £600,000 turnover, 20 per cent pre-tax return on sales); a broad strategy (for example, 'offering reliability and extra services at a price that fully reflects the value involved'); and an exit route (for example, 'selling out after five years')

5. **Risk capitalism.** At times of economic turmoil, opportunity is unusually high also. For example, redundant or squeezed-out workers with valuable skills and knowledge may well find it hard to get new jobs, especially if they're over 40, or may simply prefer the thought of being their own boss. Such people will be looking for initial seed capital, to get them under way. The sums involved are usually small – a few hundred or thousand pounds to get the business to a stage where larger investors will be interested. If you have the money available – and can afford truly to put it at risk – this can be an attractive opportunity. Basic principles:

■ *Deal in small sums only, and set a ceiling.* You should be financing just the very simplest and earliest stages of the business. Don't let yourself be sucked into an open-ended commitment. Set a ceiling of the most you'll contribute to any project, and stick to it. Also, make sure the person you're investing in is making as much of a financial commitment as possible

■ *Pay in stages.* Agree to contribute so many pounds to get the project to this stage, then so many more to get it to the next. Don't pay out the second-stage sums until you're sure the first has been completed – bringing in an outside expert to give you advice if necessary

■ *Make sure you have a written, legally binding contract before you start.* Apart from anything else, it will make dealing with subsequent investors much easier. And it will avoid the risk of falling out with your investee just as things start to come right

■ *Don't be greedy.* You can't expect too much ownership in return for your money. This is particularly important when it comes to the next stage, finding investors to take the project fully commercial. They will be putting up most of the money, so they'll want most of the ownership. That's fine, as long as you're getting the prospect of a return many times over on your original stake

■ *Don't bet on inventions.* Revolutionary new products take much longer to come to market and require far more capital than you could ever imagine. Investing in them is for people with deeper pockets. Bet on something simpler: a service business, a new way to do the same thing, a cheaper, simpler manufacturing operation. Leave the innovation to someone else

6. **House trading.** If you've got substantial equity in your house, you can cash it in and move to a bigger, potentially much more valuable property at a bargain price in a recession. Remember, though:

■ *Marginal areas are most volatile.* They go up fastest in a boom, but drop off fastest in a slump. That makes investing in a marginal area – one that's up-and-coming but hasn't yet definitely arrived – rather more of a gamble. The price may seem a bargain, but it may have further to go down before the bottom, and it may take longer to recover. In fact, since fashions change, it may never recover completely. In general, remember the basic principles of property investing – location, location, location – and try to find your bargains in areas that will always be in fashion

■ *Be financially cautious.* Leave a cushion of equity over and above the lender's minimum requirement in case prices fall further; leave a cushion, too, that will allow you to continue to meet the interest payments even if rates rise further. And don't take out bridging loans – they're too risky

■ *Buy for investment* or *personal happiness* – but try to keep the two things separate. If you're planning the move as a way of making money, don't fall in love with the house you're buying. That will blind you to its faults, lead you to overpay, and you'll probably end up pouring too much money into it to make a decent return

■ *Decorate for the target market.* Before you buy, have a clear idea of the sort of purchaser you'll sell to in a couple of years' time – and make sure you decorate with their tastes in mind, not your own

■ *Watch out for the taxman.* Although profits on selling your home are normally free of capital gains tax, that doesn't apply if the Revenue decides you've been doing it too systematically, too often and too profitably. Details from the local tax office in leaflets CGT4 and CGT8 and supplement

- *Remember that the underlying housing market may be undergoing a sea change.* Even if house prices assume their upward march, the demographics of the housing market are changing, and that means that some types of property (for example, retirement homes, mature-family houses) will be in greater demand than others (for example, first homes, yuppy flats)

7. **Searching for bargains.** If you've managed your money properly, make the most of it. When recession strikes, look out for distress sales – in shops, in second-hand stores, in tobacconists' windows. Don't be afraid to haggle to get that consumer durable or kitchen cheap. It's ghoulish, but effective.

Conclusion

When times are hard, protecting your family's assets is essential. You need to think ahead, to try to make a rational assessment of your family finances and the threats they may face. Once you've done that, you can start to take active steps to protect yourself, and to take advantage of the bad times. Remember, though, that whenever you consider an investment that's anything other than rock solid, you shouldn't invest money you can't afford to lose.

STEP 6

Shielding Your Family

The last two chapters have concentrated on the basic minimum of protection and prosperity: healthy finances. But there is more to life than that. This chapter helps you to think about your real objectives in life, and those of your family.

What do you really want?

When you're in the middle of the daily grind, or simply hoping to get to the end of the month without bouncing a cheque, it's hard to think about your real aims. In fact, it may seem unrealistic to have any but the most straightforward goals: getting by, doing a bit better next year than this, affording a better holiday, car or house.

But unless you sit down from time to time to think seriously about your long-term aims and desires, you'll never break free from the mundane. And just as important as thinking about what you'd really like is sketching a path that could take you there. This is one possible route to planning a future:

Thinking it through

1. **Fantasy time.** Find a time when you can sit down, either by yourself or with your partner, in a relaxed state to think about where you would like to be and what you would like to be doing in ten years' time. The rule of this game is that you must not let the train of thought or the conversation drift off into today's practical problems or the difficulty of achieving the aims; at the same time, you must not choose something that's preposterous ('I'd like to be King') or outside your control ('I'd like to win the Irish Sweepstakes'). Focus on things that seem unlikely, but not completely implausible: 'I'd like us to be running our own business together'; or 'I'd like us to be living in the country'; or 'I'd like to build my job around my hobby'.
   Let the thoughts flow, so that you get as completely

visualized a fantasy as possible, with all the little details fleshed out. Write it down on a piece of paper, and set the paper aside.

2. **Rejoining reality.** A day or so later, in a rather stone-cold-sober mood, sit down with the piece of paper. Now that you have a vision of how you'd like things to be, it's time to work out how to get them like that. Work backwards, a step at a time, from your end vision. What would be an easy step away from your final objective? Write it down. What would be the step before that? Write that down, too. Keep stepping back until you've got within striking distance of today's world. Fill in the gaps until you have a complete chain of not-too-taxing steps which leads from where you are to where you'd like to be.

3. **Practical planning.** The long list of steps you've written down is valuable more because it demonstrates that there is a potential chain of events leading from the present to your desired future than as a detailed blueprint for your family fortunes. The next task is to turn that potential chain into a real one. It will take time and research. You've probably made lots of assumptions about how easy it will be to get from one stage to the next; you'll need to check out how plausible those assumptions are. By the end of a few months of intermittent research and thinking, you'll probably have a much more detailed and comprehensive plan.

4. **Requirements.** At each stage there will be requirements you'll have to meet. These might be education needed, or capital required, or the perfect site for your restaurant, or a completed business plan. Go through, step by step, explicitly writing down these requirements. (You'll probably have mentioned them only implicitly up to now.) Don't let them daunt you; the longer the list the better, in some ways. Lots of medium-sized requirements that can be overcome one by one are a lot less of a barrier than a single big requirement you'll have trouble ever meeting.

5. **Milestones.** Now summarize the plan by extracting the main requirements and the date you'll have to meet them to keep

on schedule. Write them down as a series of milestones, with
dates. (If this is a family project, do it as a wall poster, in
coloured felt-tip.)

6. **The year ahead.** Write down a more detailed set of
milestones for the first year. Put that up as a wall chart, too.
Set a starting date, a week or two hence. And start. Today is
really the first day of the rest of your life.

As well as exploring what you want for yourself, think also
what you want for the rest of your family. Make sure that what
you want for them is realistic and something they'd thank you
for. There's no point in wanting your daughter to be a ballet
dancer if she spends all her time dissecting frogs; settle for
wanting a doctor in the family instead.

Then ask yourself how well your family's present life
prepares them for what you want for them, and what you can
do to change things if the answer's unsatisfactory.

The economic implications of your children's education

The best thing you can do for your children, in cold practical
terms, is to ensure that they have a good education. A child
who leaves school at the age of 15 can expect significantly
lower lifetime earnings than one who leaves school at 17. And
the 17-year-old leaver can expect lower lifetime earnings than a
child who perseveres to the equivalent of a university degree.
(Then the calculus of learning stops: you don't necessarily get
higher lifetime earnings by pressing on to do further degrees;
in fact rather the reverse, in many subjects.)

Better education isn't a recipe for happiness, of course, any
more than money is. But money certainly makes it easier to
cope with life, and education helps provide the money.

This isn't a book on how to educate your children. But any
guide to protecting your family against the worst the economic
future can hold must emphasize the value of education for this

purpose. The subject your children study is less important than that they stay at school, paying a reasonable amount of attention and passing a reasonable number of examinations, until 18 or so.

Better, of course, if they continue beyond that to university, polytechnic or technical college; better still if they leave with a qualification that will impress an employer. But the minimum you should set your sights on is staying at school to 18, with some examinations to their name. Children who manage that not-too-demanding standard have gone a long way towards making themselves permanently employable; and they have acquired enough basic education to allow them to drop back into more advanced education later on, even if they choose to drop out now.

The temptation to drop out is always strong; it will be stronger in the next decade than at any time since the 1960s. Falling numbers of young people will make competition among employers intense, bidding up starting salaries. It will be very tempting to abandon thoughts of higher education – particularly if the Government replaces grants with loans – and settle for the immediate temptations of an attractive salary and adult status. You probably won't be able to do much to persuade a determined teenager whose heart is set on joining the work force that three years in the curious limbo of student life is preferable. None the less, unless you think your child is really unsuited to higher education, it's well worth making the effort, for economic reasons if for no other ones.

The twenty-first century's seven safest careers
No career will really be safe in the twenty-first century. Already, as the twentieth century draws to a close, it's clear that the days when you joined a company at 15 and continued doing more or less the same sort of thing until you retired 50 years later have long gone. Even people who stay at the same company must expect big changes in the work they do from

one decade to the next. So someone joining the work force now can expect to have several 'careers' in the course of a lifetime.

That's good news. Changing the work you do keeps you young and alert. You bring to your new job the skills you learnt at the old; and the process of learning the new skills needed is itself rewarding and illuminating.

If skill-and-experience bundles take the place of linear career structures, some such bundles will none the less be more attractive and safer than others. So against that background, I set out rather tentatively this list of the twenty-first century's seven safest 'careers'. Notice, by the way, that they are all service industry careers. That is not white-collar snobbery, simply an obvious extrapolation of current trends. The southeast of England is already predominantly a service economy, according to the economic consultant Cambridge Econometrics; the rest of the country (and the western half of the continent) will surely follow. It makes no more sense listing manufacturing jobs as good ones for the twenty-first century than it would have done listing agricultural ones for the twentieth.

Notice also that there are no financial jobs in the list. Some financial jobs will undoubtedly be good ones; but some will be ground down as automation and electronic funds transfer makes them more and more mundane. Since it's hard to guess exactly which financial jobs will survive and which will vanish, I've left the whole category to one side.

The twenty-first century's seven safest careers

Doctor
■ The ageing of the population, and the insatiable human desire for longevity and health care will ensure a safe and prosperous future for doctors and other health workers until well into the twenty-first century. Only drastic curbs on health treatment by some future government could

prevent this scenario coming true; and even in that case doctors would at least be well-placed to ensure proper health care for themselves and their families.

Mechanical/electronic diagnostician
■ Similar forces will ensure prosperity for the twenty-first century's equivalent of the repair mechanic. Though electronic equipment will increasingly possess its own diagnostic and repair skills, the increasingly complex ways in which mechanical, electronic and human systems interact will ensure that skilled technicians will be needed to find their way through the complexities.

Designer
■ The most basic manufacturing design is dropping out of the human sphere, as computers take over tasks like laying out printed-circuit boards and doing repetitious mechanical drawing. But the need for true, human, added-value design will become ever more marked, in every activity from packaging to retailing, advertising and consumer goods. Making things look and feel good; adding imagination and flair to the mundane; bringing drama and excitement to the commercial environment – all these are the roles of the twenty-first century designer, for whom there will always be a career.

Editor
■ Information will be the raw material of the twenty-first century economy. Or rather, information will be what the economy *needs*. What it *gets* will be something quite different: data, which stands in relation to information as lumps of coal do to electric current. In between the two, the power station of the twenty-first century, stands the unlikely figure of the editor. Making sense of numbers and words, marshalling facts into argument, tidying up prose for an increasingly illiterate world: all these basic editorial skills will be increasingly valuable, under a range of different job titles, to a surprisingly wide collection of industries and institutions. Good editing is the result of an ordered mind and a set of mental disciplines; to be really useful, it needs to go along with specific knowledge of a

subject or area of expertise. So twenty-first century editing will be the domain of well-educated people from every discipline with a flair for language and clarity.

Gene engineer
■ The ability to adjust genes to produce biologically superior organisms, already partly with us, will be one of the twenty-first century's growth industries. Not just for human organisms, of course; for plants, other animals and microbe-level 'agents' as well. The technology will pervade every industry, just as electronics and computer technology did in the twentieth century.

Salesperson
■ Even if day-to-day transactions become automated (as they already are for such tasks as buying petrol or using the office coffee machine), the need for salespeople will remain a staple feature of twenty-first century life. Creative selling of high-price, high-margin products will continue to be a human monopoly, since it requires those characteristics of empathy, theatre and guile which are hardest to render artificially. (And this will increasingly be an area where women have their fair share of the jobs, as they already do in the American sales force.) But there will also be well-paid jobs in retail sales. Retailing will separate into two tiers: one increasingly automated for routine transactions; and one relying heavily on personal service to make shopping a pleasure again. In the 'routine' tier, unskilled, discontented, low-paid salespeople will vanish, to be replaced by machines. In the 'service' tier, relatively well-educated, well-paid sales assistants will bring grace and drama to a side of retailing that is more a leisure activity than a chore.

Servant
■ Wealthy people want personal service, and are prepared to make enormous concessions to get it. Money is one concession; autonomy and respect are others. Increasingly, as the population gets older and richer, there will be a rising demand for personal services. There will be, correspondingly, a growing willingness on the part of

employers to pay the necessary price of treating the new generation of servants as independent spirits performing a skilled and indispensable task. Not everyone will want to enter service, even on the new, far more equitable terms. But for those who possess the necessary patience and tact, it will certainly be one of the twenty-first century's safest careers.

Protecting your partner

These days only a minority of British households are the sort seen on the television commercials: father out working, mother at home, two kids. An increasingly large proportion of households consist of working couples, with or without children, and with or without the benefit of matrimony.

In such circumstances, the traditional approach to family protection – dad takes out insurance policy payable to mum – is of limited value. Depending on your circumstances, you may find the following approaches helpful:

Five ways of protecting your family

1. **Don't die intestate.** Whatever your relationship, write a will. People who die intestate – without making a will – are letting their surviving family in for a quite unnecessary amount of hardship. Sorting out the financial affairs of someone who dies intestate is a messy business – the last thing you want your grieving family to have to cope with. Worse, the final result may be very unsatisfactory – not at all what you'd have wanted had you set down your thoughts on the matter. This can be true even if you're married. For example, you might want all the assets – insurance policy, house, everything – to go to your spouse. But if you have children, that isn't how the law works. Part is set aside in trust for them, and in the worst circumstances, that can lead to the house being sold. If you're not married, things can be even messier. You can get a standard will form from legal stationers that will – if correctly signed and witnessed – at least ensure you don't die intestate. A will tailored more closely to your individual needs and

desires is a bit more complicated; a solicitor will draw one up, though the process will go much more smoothly if you've thought through who you want to leave things to in advance. (Note: the rules on intestacy are different in Scotland; but it's still not desirable to die without leaving a will. And wherever you live, remember that changing circumstances will affect the provisions of your will, so revise it relatively frequently.)

2. **Getting at the money.** Make sure your bank accounts are accessible. Many couples, in particular unmarried ones, have elaborate bank account arrangements – one bank account each for cheques and one for the house; one building society account each for savings and one for the house. That's fine (as long as you can juggle the cash flow between them), but it's important not to inadvertently leave important lumps of cash in an account your partner doesn't have access to. When you die, the bank immediately seals your account; if your partner can't write cheques on it, he or she can't get at money which may be urgently needed to meet the household bills. Again, the last thing your family needs is to have to scrabble frantically for cash to meet standing orders and other household expenses at a time when they're also trying to cope with grief. Joint accounts (of the sort that can be drawn on by the survivor) get round the problem. You can still have a number of them, to allow you to run separate finances, with an understanding that they're to be treated as 'my' account and 'your' account unless something dreadful happens. You may, none the less, have reasons for not wanting your partner to have access to your bank accounts – but at least you shouldn't stumble into this sort of problem without thinking of the implications. Serious sickness, by the way, can pose just as many problems in this area as death.

3. **Unwedded bliss.** If you're not married, draw up an agreement. Marriages can end just as abruptly as unmarried relationships – but married couples have access to a body of rules, the divorce laws, which decide who gets what when the partnership is over. Unmarried couples have no such body of legislation to sort out their affairs. And because unmarried couples usually move into a long-term relationship stage by stage, the various bits of property they've accumulated may

have a legal status that doesn't entirely match up to the implicit understandings of settling down together. Alas, such implicit understandings rarely survive the collapse of a relationship, particularly if it's an acrimonious rupture, and the partners are thrown back on legal niceties – which may give one partner no share in a house he or she always thought of as a joint arrangement. The best solution is a legal contract covering shared assets of the partnership. It's terribly unromantic, however, and relatively few people can bring themselves to go through such a rigmarole in the first flush of love. And after that, of course, it becomes a little delicate . . . If you can't bring yourself to suggest that the new love of your life meet you at the solicitor before bringing round a toothbrush, at least make sure that any house purchase, mortgage, and so on is done jointly in both names. That will resolve one potential problem. But, unromantic though it is, a contract is better still.

4. **Take out insurance.** Once you have children, you need some form of life insurance, probably for both of you. A family in which one person goes out to work while the other runs the house and looks after the children needs two insurance policies, just as much as where both parents go out to work. Protection-only term insurance, the simplest form of life insurance, will meet this need. It covers you against death or injury for a specific period of time (say to retirement). At the end of that period, the coverage simply stops, with no further benefits. Term assurance is relatively cheap, particularly if you actively search out those companies that specialize in providing it at low cost. You can find listings of the cheapest reputable companies in this field in *Investors Chronicle*, *Money Which* and *Money Management*. If you're buying this sort of policy from an insurance agent, you may find that he or she tries to sell you a more elaborate 'endowment' policy, one which gives you a lump sum at the end of the term as well. (You may already be using this sort of policy as part of your mortgage arrangements.) Endowment policies are a popular form of saving – but if all you want is insurance against death or injury, rather than a savings medium, protection-only term assurance will meet the need.

Increasingly, life assurance companies are starting to worry about AIDS and its impact on their male policyholders. If your answers on the policy-proposal form lead the insurance company to think you might belong to a high-risk group, it may insist on an HIV test before issuing the policy.

If the policy is to be taken out on the life of a partner who looks after the home and the children, make sure you calculate the appropriate sum correctly. What you may well need, particularly if the children are young, is an annuity large enough to cover the costs of 1½ people – enough to cover child care for the hours between leaving home and coming back in the evening, together with housekeeping and house cleaning services. Insurance cover big enough to buy all that may, in fact, be prohibitively expensive – but at least if you start out with a realistic idea of the survivor's burden, you have a better estimate of the cover to settle for.

5. **Steer company benefits properly.** If your company offers death-in-service insurance protection as part of the pension scheme, you may choose not to make independent insurance arrangements, but to rely on that. If you do, make sure that the trustees of the pension scheme, who will have to pay out any death benefit, know whom you want the money to go. For married couples, that's usually obvious; for unmarried couples or ones where one or the other partner is divorced, there can be no end of problems. These can all be avoided by letting the company know who you wish to be the beneficiary. Most companies circulate forms for this purpose from time to time, but a surprisingly large number of people fail to fill them in – leading to much embarrassment on the part of the trustees when they have to decide between the claims of former and current partners, and occasionally real hardship for one or the other of them. Once again, this can be avoided by letting the company know who should receive the benefit of the policy.

Making the most of a legacy

Until recently, for most people legacies were things that happened in the final acts of Victorian melodrama, or consisted of a gold watch and a few yellowing War Loan certificates. The increase in house ownership, and the relentless rise in property prices, has changed all that. It has ensured that many people born in the baby-bulge years after the Second World War will be receiving far more substantial legacies than anything their parents could have imagined.

The figures are most striking in the south-east of England, where property prices are highest. Two baby-boom siblings inheriting a suburban house would share, say, £160,000 between them – £80,000 each. (For the purpose of this example I've assumed that the parents order their affairs well enough to avoid inheritance-tax on their estates.) Since each of the siblings is likely to be married, their families might receive legacies from two sets of parents, doubling the size of the windfall. £160,000 is a substantial sum of money, particularly when it goes to middle-aged families already well down the road of house-purchase. If the couple inheriting this sum did no more than preserve it against the ravages of inflation till they reached retirement age, then used it to buy an annuity from an insurance company, it would provide them an income of £14,000 a year for as long as either of them lived.

What is a sensible approach to take with a legacy? Particularly at a time of persistent inflation, it is important to take some specific action, and not simply let a legacy slip away, worn down by rising prices and household expenditures. Here is a possible approach to a legacy:

Set aside some mad-money. Decide right at the outset that a portion – perhaps a very small one – will be dedicated to extravagance. If you don't set any money aside in this way, but earmark all the legacy for sensible purposes, such as the children's education or repairing the roof, you will feel frustrated once the money's spent and tempted to wreck your ordinary household budget to give yourself treats you sacrificed earlier. Equally, if you don't set a firm ceiling on your extravagance money, you run the risk that the whole legacy will be swallowed up in pleasant but ultimately unrewarding ways. It's a good idea to separate out this money at an early stage, perhaps by transferring it to another account, so as to leave the bulk of the legacy untouched.

Pay down debt. Consider paying off some of your high-interest debt. If you are paying 30 per cent or more interest (as on some credit cards, particularly those from stores), you should consider paying it off: as an investment, this represents a higher guaranteed rate of return than you can get anywhere else. However, if you know you'll simply end up running up credit-card bills that will soon take you back to the same level of indebtedness, paying them off probably isn't a good idea. It would simply be a disguised way of funnelling more of your legacy into day-to-day consumption – something you'll probably want to avoid. If you can be confident you won't go back into high-interest debt, however, paying it off represents a sensible use of part of your legacy.

Hold back on the house. Be very careful about splurging on building work on the house. By all means spend money on re-doing the kitchen, or adding a conservatory if you intend to make use of them. But don't view them as investments; it's very hard to get your money back on such additions when the time comes to sell the house. What decides the relative price of your house will be some very basic facts, like location and number of bedrooms. Elaborate decoration or extensions that don't add to the number of bedrooms may make the house sell a bit quicker, but they won't have a big impact on the price you receive. (And even the selling-quicker argument isn't always effective – for every potential buyer who can't resist the gold ceiling in the living room, there'll be another who's rendered speechless and unenthusiastic.)

Consider reducing your mortgage if you want more flexibility. You can use a legacy to pay down or pay off your mortgage. In general, it is not a good idea to reduce your mortgage below the level at which it attracts maximum tax relief on the interest you pay. There are permanent rumours about Budget changes to mortgage interest tax relief, so make sure you know the exact ceiling and other rules in force at the time before you make any final decision on this subject. This tax relief is a valuable privilege, powerful enough to turn a positive real interest rate (you paying them) into a negative one ('them' – that is, the building society and your fellow taxpayers – paying you interest on every pound you borrow up to the mortgage tax relief ceiling). It would be a pity to give this up, unless you have particular reasons for wishing to be free of debt. However, *reducing* your mortgage, perhaps to the tax relief ceiling, is another matter. Factors to take into account when considering this course of action include:

- Any restrictions or penalties for early repayment of your mortgage. (Some lenders waive such penalties within six months after a mortgage rate increase, so even if you can't redeem the mortgage cost-free today, you may be able to do so in a few months' time.)
- Whether you have an endowment mortgage or a conventional one. If you have an endowment mortgage, it may well be in your interests to keep making the payments on the policy even after the mortgage has been redeemed or reduced. These sorts of policy can usually attract unfavourable terms if they are terminated early. This calculation may affect the attractiveness of reducing or redeeming the mortgage.
- The implicit rate of return from reducing your mortgage payments compared with the return you can get elsewhere. Remember to compare like with like: in a real bonanza year, you might get a 20–30 per cent total return on an investment in

the stock market. But that return is riskier than the one you get from reducing your mortgage. More predictable investments would be hard put to match the 14–15 per cent after-tax you could get in early 1990 from mortgage reduction.

■ How much you need flexibility. Once you've paid down your mortgage, you may not be able to turn that money back into spending power again until you sell the house – it depends on someone else lending against the value of it. So a decision to pay down a mortgage makes your asset portfolio even more biased towards house ownership than it already is. That shouldn't stop you using some of the money to pay down the mortgage, if the comparison of returns looks favourable. Equally, though, you shouldn't necessarily expect to pay off quite as much as if the returns calculation were the only thing that mattered. Diversification matters too.

■ A yearning for freedom. The discipline of meeting monthly mortgage payments is a stringent one. It may well force you to keep doing a job you hate, or close off the option of starting up on your own – simply because you cannot guarantee being able to meet the monthly mortgage payments on time if you make the change. Reducing (or even eliminating) the mortgage can have a liberating influence here, quite outstripping any purely financial calculations.

Search for appropriate financial advice. Willy-nilly, financial advisers in Britain have been separated into two camps: those who act as the tied outlet of a particular financial institution or group of such houses; and those who are not tied to any particular supplier, picking and choosing from those products available. Each of these groups receives commission – sometimes a very substantial one – on what they sell, and the new City regulatory regime now allows you to find out what proportion of your initial payments will be going in commission.

There are two other groups offering assistance: one is the salaried-sales force of those insurance companies and investment houses that prefer to operate through their own staff rather than independents. (You can't find out how much these sales forces cost their employers, much to the chagrin of those institutions that operate through the – now much more transparent – commission system.)

The other group, into which many professional people such as lawyers and accountants fall, offer independent advice, without taking any commission from suppliers of financial products; or at any rate by setting them off against their own fees.

This increasing polarization is the result of changes in the regulations governing the sale of financial services, and of an increasingly competitive atmosphere among providers. The result, however, can be confusing. Before you decide on an adviser, find out just how independent he or she is.

Aim for a diversified portfolio of assets. Whether you are relying on advice or trying to make all the decisions yourself, it is important to avoid putting all your eggs in one basket. This can be frustrating, when you see one particular part of your portfolio – your house, for example, or shares – racing ahead while the others languish. But, over the sort of time that most people are interested in – the 20 to 40-year hauls of building up assets for retirement, or getting the children started in life – diversified holdings have the attraction of steadiness. A diversified portfolio might include some or all of the following:

■ Property (your home).

- Shares (held directly or through unit trusts).
- Fixed interest investments (gilt-edged securities from the UK Government, for example, National Savings Certificates, or an income bond from an insurance company).
- Floating-rate deposits (for example, a 90-day high-interest account at a building society or a money-market account).

The share portion of the portfolio might itself be subdivided into a large chunk held 'passively', perhaps in the sort of unit trust that attempts to mimic the movements of the whole range of shares available, and a smaller portion managed 'actively', either by you taking a flutter or by investing in the more aggressive unit trusts that offer high potential rewards and correspondingly higher risks.

You might want to consider diversifying by country as well as by investment type, but if you ultimately plan to use your nest-egg in the UK, most advisers would recommend that the bulk of it should be held in sterling, because that is the currency in which you intend to spend it.

Protecting your protection

Most of the principles in this chapter apply as much when times are good as when they're uncertain: the penalty for not writing a will doesn't change whether the economy's booming or sliding quietly into a recession. (If you do plan to invest a legacy, however, bear in mind the five threats to wealth listed in Step 4.)

When the economic climate is unsettled, however, the policies of protection and caution touched on in this chapter seem, if anything, more pointed and relevant.

None the less, such an approach shouldn't stop you sitting down to try to plan a longer-term future that is much more ambitious than anything you've considered up till now.

STEP 7

Reducing the Retirement Risks

A large part of most people's economic planning is concerned with preparing for a happy and prosperous retirement. When economic conditions are uncertain or unpromising, retirement planning becomes particularly challenging.

There are two basic, motherhood-and-apple-pie rules:

You can't begin too soon

and

Every little helps

These two principles are both directly relevant to troubled economic times. To rephrase them, in the context of a recession:

- Don't let economic difficulties lead you to put off preparing for retirement, even if you can only make a small contribution to start with.
- Even if you have to reduce the amount you're putting aside towards retirement, do keep making some contribution towards your future, however small.

And at times when inflation is a serious worry, you can add a third principle to the two above:

- NEVER underestimate the damage that even a small rise in the long-term rate of inflation can do to your hopes and plans. (If you have any doubts about that point, re-read the section on inflation as a threat to your family wealth, on page 142.)

We'll be exploring the implications of these principles for the rest of the chapter. But in the next recession – and indeed for the rest of your working and retired life – you'll have to grapple with an additional factor.

Nigel Lawson's legacy: the pensions minefield

Actually, it isn't really fair to call it Nigel Lawson's legacy: he shares responsibility for the complete transformation of the pensions outlook in the second half of the 1980s with another now-departed Conservative minister, Sir Norman Fowler.

Between them, as Chancellor of the Exchequer and Secretary of State for Health and Social Services respectively, they changed a predictable, if often rather unfair, selection of pensions choices into a much richer, potentially much more rewarding, set of options.

But freedom to choose implies freedom to choose wrongly, and the new options opened up for people preparing for retirement include some that will lead to regrets later in life.

The new pensions gospel contains a number of brisk new truths, many of which have not fully been appreciated by most people:

Don't feel quite so hard done by when you change jobs ...
It's harder for the employer to give you a raw deal when you depart, though you're still not as well off in pension terms as someone who stays put.

... But watch out for catch-22. If you move from a job in which you joined the pension scheme before June 1989, the fine-print of the tax rules imposes some unattractive restrictions on how the pension at your new job may be paid out. That also applies if you first join a pension scheme after that date.

You now have the chance to create a 'personal pension' ... Your employer can't force you to join a company pension scheme, and you can gain the same tax advantages by setting up your own personal pension, which you carry with you from job to job. The chances are your employer won't contribute to it, however, unless you make it part of your negotiations at the outset. Still, a personal pension can be based around your idea of when it would be a good time to retire, rather than your employer's.

... But if you do, you must start to think quite differently about pensions provision. A personal pension, like a small, but growing, number of company pensions, will be a 'money purchase' scheme, rather than the 'final salary' type that most firms offer. This means that you'll get the pension your contributions have paid for – which will bear no particular relationship to your final salary. You must calculate much more carefully what the return on your pension plan is likely to be, and how that compares with expected inflation. And you won't be able to rely on the benevolence of the pension scheme trustees to give you a bit of a boost if inflation starts to nibble away at your income when you're a pensioner.

You have lots of new opportunities to build up your pension in a tax-sheltered way ... For example, even if you're in a company pension scheme, you can set up a sort of personal pension on the side, through a particular type of top-up pension payment, known as a 'Free-Standing Additional Voluntary Contribution'. You can choose pretty much any kind of investment for this purpose, including making your own share picks.

... But some of those choices will be much less advantageous than others, and it's up to you to sort them out. Lots of investment institutions are repackaging their usual products as glossy new Personal Pensions or Free-Standing Additional Voluntary Contributions. Some of these are fine for the purpose; some are suitable for short-term saving, but not for building up a long-term pension fund; and others are just not a very good deal. *Caveat emptor.*

Don't put too much faith in the state . . . In case you were expecting the State Earnings Related Pension Scheme, announced with much fanfare in the 1970s, to solve all your pension problems, think again. As part of the new reforms, it's being run down and has intentionally been made less attractive for people retiring after 1998. There are a complicated set of decisions to make as to whether you'll be better off 'contracting out' of the scheme, if you haven't done so already.

. . . And finally, watch out for catch-23. As well as the catch-22 mentioned above, there's an even nastier one that could affect many people if inflation continues. This puts a ceiling on the amount of salary that you can use as the basis for tax-sheltered pension contributions. In early 1990, it was £60,000 a year, and it rises in line with price inflation, so it might not sound as if it affects many people. But average wages rise by two or three per cent more each year than inflation, and you may well be expecting a more rapid increase than that if the best years of your career lie ahead. With an average annual pay increase, including promotions, of four per cent more than inflation, someone aged 30 earning £25,000 a year now could be up against the ceiling in 22 years' time, at the age of 52. Once the ceiling applies to you, you'll have to pay tax on any pension contributions you or your employer make in respect of the portion of your salary that's over the ceiling – sharply reducing the attractiveness of saving through a pension scheme. One saving grace: the ceiling only applies to someone changing jobs after mid-1989. But what happens if you want to change jobs between now and retirement? And – catch-23a – a similar ceiling applies to personal pensions.

To get the full story on the opportunities and problems that the new pension system promises, you'll have to read one of the many good books on the subject. In the rest of this chapter, however, I'll attempt to sketch the central decisions you'll have to make in preparing for your retirement – and how a recession or other bad economic news affects them.

How much will I need when I retire?

Calculating how much you need to save for a satisfactory retirement is a complicated job, since you have to grapple with the state pension system, your own company pension, your expectations and the likely future course of inflation. Before settling down to do these estimates, it's a good idea to have to hand your company pension scheme details, and an estimate of your current living expenses, such as the one outlined in Step 3. Set aside a clear evening – preferably one on which you're not feeling too depressed – and settle down to the following exercise.

The first question, obviously, is what sort of a life you plan to live when you retire. The budgeting exercise in Step 3 will give you a good idea of your current expenditure; you must now modify it to take account of how you expect things to change when you retire. Likely changes include:

- Savings on expenditures connected with your job: travel to work, lunches, work clothes, pension contributions, tax.
- Savings to do with family life – the departure of the children, and so on.
- Savings to do with moving, if you plan to move to a smaller house or a cheaper area on retirement. (You should also allow for the fact that your mortgage could well be paid off by the time you retire.)

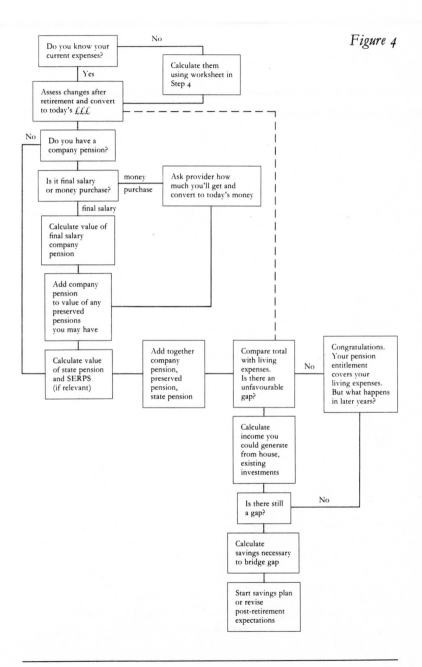

Figure 4

- Expenditure to do with leisure pursuits (golf, other games, the theatre, eating out). Expenditure to do with extra travel for pleasure.
- Expenditure to do with a car, if you've always had a company car up till now.
- Expenditure to do with health, including the need perhaps for extra assistance on chores, such as cleaning and gardening as they become more of a burden.

That leads on to the next question . . .

How much can I count on already?

Once you've got a rough figure, in today's pounds, of how much income you'd need if you retired tomorrow, the first question you must ask is whether your company pension would provide that living standard.

Company pension. Ask the company pensions department to calculate how much you'll get based on how many years of service you'll have when you reach retirement. There are a number of wrinkles, however:

Calculating your pension from work

1. **Lump sum.** You will be able to take a portion of your pension in the form of a tax-free lump sum (up to the limits the tax man allows). You'll probably find this worthwhile, since, for tax and other reasons, you may well be able to use it to generate a better income than the pension scheme offers. For the purpose of this calculation, however, treat that as a bonus; what we're trying to calculate is the money you can be sure of when you retire, and the final-salary calculation is the best first estimate.

2. **'Money purchase' schemes.** If you have a personal pension, rather than a company one, you'll have to calculate

how big an annual income it will provide at retirement. The person who sold it to you should be able to help in this calculation.

You will probably have been given two estimates of the pension you'll get, based on two different estimates of how well the underlying investments on which the pension is based perform between now and your retirement. Your actual pension won't bear any relation to these estimates, of course; it will solely depend on how well or badly the pension manager invests between now and the time, perhaps well into the twenty-first century, when you turn up to collect. Still, the two calculations (at officially-mandated rates of return of 8.5 per cent and 13.5 per cent) are your best starting point for calculating how much you will get. To be on the safe side, do most of your calculations on the basis of the lower amount; you can tantalize yourself by looking at the higher one as well if you like, but be very cautious about taking it seriously. If the quotation you've been given is in terms of a lump sum at retirement, with which to purchase an annuity (a guaranteed annual pension for the rest of your life), see page 209 for the calculations that will turn that into an annual income.

These sums will be in money of the day, of course, not the real terms we're using for the rest of this calculation. To convert the retirement figure to today's money, multiply it by the appropriate number from Table 5, below. Similar principles apply if you're a member of a money purchase company scheme, rather than a final salary one. And they are also likely to apply to Additional Voluntary Contributions (extra payments you make to boost your company pension) and Free-Standing Additional Voluntary Contributions (extra payments you make to build an additional pension on the side).

Table 5 **How much a future sum (or annuity) will be worth in today's money**

To calculate how much a future annuity will be worth each year in today's money, multiply the amount you're expecting by the factor appropriate to your retirement date. Use a similar calculation to work

---

out the value in today's money of an expected future lump sum. Use the column for the inflation rate you expect.

Year of retirement	Inflation rate between now and then			
	3.5%	5%	7%	9%
1990	1.00	1.00	1.00	1.00
1991	0.97	0.95	0.93	0.92
1992	0.93	0.91	0.87	0.84
1993	0.90	0.86	0.82	0.77
1994	0.87	0.82	0.76	0.71
1995	0.84	0.78	0.71	0.65
1996	0.81	0.75	0.67	0.60
1997	0.79	0.71	0.62	0.55
1998	0.76	0.68	0.58	0.50
1999	0.73	0.64	0.54	0.46
2000	0.71	0.61	0.51	0.42
2001	0.68	0.58	0.48	0.39
2002	0.66	0.56	0.44	0.36
2003	0.64	0.53	0.41	0.33
2004	0.62	0.51	0.39	0.30
2005	0.60	0.48	0.36	0.27
2006	0.58	0.46	0.34	0.25
2007	0.56	0.44	0.32	0.23
2008	0.54	0.42	0.30	0.21
2009	0.52	0.40	0.28	0.19
2010	0.50	0.38	0.26	0.18
2011	0.49	0.36	0.24	0.16
2012	0.47	0.34	0.23	0.15
2013	0.45	0.33	0.21	0.14
2014	0.44	0.31	0.20	0.13
2015	0.42	0.30	0.18	0.12
2016	0.41	0.28	0.17	0.11
2017	0.40	0.27	0.16	0.10
2018	0.38	0.26	0.15	0.09

Year of retirement	Inflation rate between now and then			
	3.5%	*5%*	*7%*	*9%*
2019	0.37	0.24	0.14	0.08
2020	0.36	0.23	0.13	0.08
2021	0.34	0.22	0.12	0.07
2022	0.33	0.21	0.11	0.06
2023	0.32	0.20	0.11	0.06
2024	0.31	0.19	0.10	0.05
2025	0.30	0.18	0.09	0.05
2026	0.29	0.17	0.09	0.04
2027	0.28	0.16	0.08	0.04
2028	0.27	0.16	0.08	0.04
2029	0.26	0.15	0.07	0.03
2030	0.25	0.14	0.07	0.03
2031	0.24	0.14	0.06	0.03
2032	0.24	0.13	0.06	0.03
2033	0.23	0.12	0.05	0.02
2034	0.22	0.12	0.05	0.02
2035	0.21	0.11	0.05	0.02

3. **Preserved pension.** If you have a preserved pension from a previous job, you should have been told how much pension you'd qualified for by the time you left. By law, a preserved pension earned after 1984 has to be increased each year in line with the Retail Prices Index – up to a maximum of five per cent a year. Some employers may be more generous than that, and some may apply uprating to years of service before 1985. Since there's a good chance that inflation will average five per cent or more over the next generation, you may well get less in real terms from a preserved pension than the amount you were entitled to when you left. This is especially true if much of your service was before 1984, and even more so if much of it was before the big inflation of the late 1970s.

If you're due to retire soon, you'll be able to do more accurate calculations about how much your preserved pension is worth fairly simply. If you're not due to retire for ten years or so, you should treat any preserved pension owing for pre-1985 years of service as a pleasant surprise rather than something to count on (unless the pension fund has promised to uprate it to offset inflation). And you should downgrade your entitlement to a preserved pension earned after 1985 a bit, to reflect the chances that inflation will be higher than the government-mandated uprating.

These calculations should give you the pre-tax income you'd have from your (present or previous) company scheme if your retirement date were tomorrow.

State pension. Now add to it the basic state pension: £43.60 (in early 1990) for a single person who'd made enough contributions to qualify for the full amount; £69.80 for a married man. That's £2266.20 a year for a single person, £3629.60 for a married man. You may also qualify for up to £4 a week or so from the old graduated pension scheme, which ended in 1975.

SERPS. If you're not contracted out of the State Earnings Related Pension Scheme (SERPS), you'll qualify for a payment from that. (The company pension scheme documents will tell you whether you're contracted out or not.) If you're still in SERPS, the exact amount you get will depend on your average earnings from 1978 to your state pension age, up to a maximum (in today's money) of £3,666. If your state pension age arrives in 1999 or later, the maximum SERPS payment will be less, though it won't drop below £2,932 a year in today's money. To qualify for a maximum SERPS pension, you have to have average pre-tax earnings, in today's money, of £16,900 a year, £325 a week. For the purposes of this calculation, guesstimate what proportion of the maximum payment you'll be entitled to, allowing for how your average salary (excluding inflation) is likely to compare with the £16,900 figure. It won't be completely accurate, but it will be close enough for this purpose.

First stab. You should now be able to take a first stab at estimating how well the combination of your state pension entitlement and your company or personal pension compared with your estimate of how much you'll need at retirement. All the calculations have been done in today's money, assuming you retired tomorrow, which is a convenient way of factoring inflation out of the equation.

Second thoughts. If you're anything like me, you'll be horrified by the results. Still, your state and company pensions won't be the only thing you'll be able to rely on. You'll also have the proceeds of any investments or other savings, and if you plan to sell your house and move to a smaller one, the proceeds of that transaction.

So the next step in the calculation is to work out what your investments, money purchase pensions or assets will be worth at your retirement date, and calculate how much of a monthly payment they will provide for you. If it weren't for inflation, that would be relatively simple. Alas, it isn't. So take it step by step, still doing the calculations in terms of today's money.

The first thing is to calculate how big your assets will be when you retire. Start by adding them up.

Adding up the assets

1. **The profit you make on your house.** To be really conservative, you could assume that house prices stay constant in real terms between now and retirement. If that's so, the profit can be calculated easily enough by taking the current value of your house (this time you don't need to assume a hurried sale – use the figure you'd be likely to get if you could take your time looking for a buyer) and subtracting from it the price of the house or flat you would move into.

   However, house prices have risen in real terms for so long that (despite the fears about the long-run prospect for the housing market outlined on page 152) most people are likely to assume some real increase in prices between now and retirement.

The simplest way to allow for that is to take the profit you'd make if house prices stayed constant in real terms (as calculated above) and then increase it in line with the rate by which you expect house prices to outstrip the general level of inflation. Do that by choosing such a rate (3.5 or five per cent) from Table 6, below, then use the multiplication factor appropriate for your retirement date to calculate the value of the profit then.

Table 6 **How to calculate the value of a house that grows at a steady rate in real terms**

This table can be used to estimate the value of a house or any other asset which grows at a steady rate in real terms. Choose the column appropriate to the rate at which the asset grows in value (3.5 per cent or five per cent is the highest rate you are likely to see on a consistent basis in real terms). Then read off its value (assuming the growth occurs) at your retirement. The table can also be used to calculate growth in nominal values, of course.

Year of retirement	Factor to multiply by			
	3.5%	5%	7%	9%
1990	1.00	1.00	1.00	1.00
1991	1.03	1.05	1.07	1.09
1992	1.07	1.10	1.14	1.19
1993	1.11	1.16	1.23	1.30
1994	1.15	1.22	1.31	1.41
1995	1.19	1.28	1.40	1.54
1996	1.23	1.34	1.50	1.68
1997	1.27	1.41	1.61	1.83
1998	1.32	1.48	1.72	1.99

Year of retirement	3.5%	Factor to multiply by 5%	7%	9%
1999	1.36	1.55	1.84	2.17
2000	1.41	1.63	1.97	2.37
2001	1.46	1.71	2.10	2.58
2002	1.51	1.80	2.25	2.81
2003	1.56	1.89	2.41	3.07
2004	1.62	1.98	2.58	3.34
2005	1.68	2.08	2.76	3.64
2006	1.73	2.18	2.95	3.97
2007	1.79	2.29	3.16	4.33
2008	1.86	2.41	3.38	4.72
2009	1.92	2.53	3.62	5.14
2010	1.99	2.65	3.87	5.60
2011	2.06	2.79	4.14	6.11
2012	2.13	2.93	4.43	6.66
2013	2.21	3.07	4.74	7.26
2014	2.28	3.23	5.07	7.91
2015	2.36	3.39	5.43	8.62
2016	2.45	3.56	5.81	9.40
2017	2.53	3.73	6.21	10.25
2018	2.62	3.92	6.65	11.17
2019	2.71	4.12	7.11	12.17
2020	2.81	4.32	7.61	13.27
2021	2.91	4.54	8.15	14.46
2022	3.01	4.76	8.72	15.76
2023	3.11	5.00	9.33	17.18
2024	3.22	5.25	9.98	18.73
2025	3.33	5.52	10.68	20.41
2026	3.45	5.79	11.42	22.25
2027	3.57	6.08	12.22	24.25
2028	3.70	6.39	13.08	26.44
2029	3.83	6.70	13.99	28.82
2030	3.96	7.04	14.97	31.41

Year of retirement	3.5%	Factor to multiply by 5%	7%	9%
2031	4.10	7.39	16.02	34.24
2032	4.24	7.76	17.14	37.32
2033	4.39	8.15	18.34	40.68
2034	4.54	8.56	19.63	44.34
2035	4.70	8.99	21.00	48.33

How inflation affects the income you'll need

This table can also be used to calculate the pension you'll need at your retirement date to give you the same pre-tax salary, in real terms, today (early 1990).

To use it, multiply your current pre-tax salary by the factor appropriate to your retirement year, choosing the column that reflects the average long-run inflation rate you expect over the period.

---

2. Financial assets. These include investments (shares, unit trusts, gilts), savings accounts, and so on, plus the terminal value of any endowment insurance policies. Here again you need to calculate how much these will be worth in real terms, on your retirement. If the salesperson has given you an estimate, use that, adjusting it downwards – if it's expressed in money-of-the-day terms – by multiplying by the appropriate factor from Table 5 on page 199. If he or she hasn't given you an estimate, do it yourself, assuming a 3.5 per cent long-run real return.

If you expect to save the same amount every year, in real terms, use Table 7, below, to calculate how much that will accumulate if you're able to achieve a 3.5 per cent rate of return after inflation.

Table 7 **How much an annual rate of saving will bring**

This table can be used to calculate how much annual savings of £1,000 will be worth by the time they've accumulated at a real rate of return.

Assume you start saving in year 1, and cash the investments in at your retirement.

Years to retirement	Real rate of return: 3.5%
1	1,000
2	2,035
3	3,106
4	4,215
5	5,362
6	6,550
7	7,779
8	9,052
9	10,368
10	11,731
11	13,142
12	14,602
13	16,113
14	17,677
15	19,296
16	20,971
17	22,705
18	24,500
19	26,357
20	28,280
21	30,269
22	32,329
23	34,460
24	36,667
25	38,950
26	41,313
27	43,759
28	46,291
29	48,911
30	51,623

Years to retirement	*Real rate of return: 3.5%*
31	54,429
32	57,335
33	60,341
34	63,453
35	66,674
36	70,008
37	73,458
38	77,029
39	80,725
40	84,550

A real rate of return of 3.5 per cent may not seem ambitious, but in fact it requires making some fairly sensible judgements about the place you put your savings. If you're being offered a higher rate of return, you're almost certainly being asked to take a higher level of risk in order to achieve it; and over a sustained period of time, that risk factor can prove very painful.

A 3.5 per cent real rate of return is an even more demanding target if you're having to pay tax on the interest or dividends you receive on your investments, or on the capital gains. In fact, you should probably only expect to get a 3.5 per cent real rate of return on savings you can protect from the taxman, such as pension contributions (including Voluntary Contributions) and Personal Equity Plans (see page 162). On other savings, you should expect the effective real rate of return to be reduced by tax.

3. **And don't forget . . .** You may also have a potential retirement nest-egg that you've forgotten about. If you are using an endowment policy to pay off your house mortgage, and if it's of the 'with profits' sort, it will be generating earnings over and above the amount you'll need to meet the mortgage. Dig out a recent profits entitlement statement from the insurance company, and try to work out what the likely end-payment will be. Then subtract the cost of the mortgage

and turn the resulting sum into today's money by using Table 5 on page 199. Also add in any long-service bonus or other retirement golden handshake you can expect from your employer.

At this point you will have a rough calculation of the value, in today's money, of any lump sums you can look forward to on retirement. That will allow you to go on to calculate the annuity (or lifetime annual pension) that such a lump sum would buy. In February 1990, the following were the best annuity rates quoted by *Money Management* magazine:

▶ For a single man, retiring at 65, a £10,000 lump sum would buy a lifetime annuity of £1,494.20 a year. For a single woman, retiring at 60, £10,000 would buy an annuity of £1,270.00. And if the two of them were a couple, £10,000 would buy £1,210.00 a year that would last until both of them had died.

Life expectancy increases over time, so the annuity any given sum will buy can be expected to drop between now and the time you retire. Also, annuity rates depend on the interest rate on long-term government bonds; when those rates are high annuity rates are favourable for the purchaser. When interest rates drop away, they are less generous. So don't count on favourable rates at your retirement date.

Nothing says you have to buy an annuity when you retire, of course (except for a personal pension, when the taxman forces you to buy one). In fact, when you first retire, an annuity may not be very attractive; you could achieve the same rate of return from other sources, and still keep your capital. As you get older, an insurance company annuity becomes a better bet. The calculation of an annuity is useful, however, because it shows how much you'd get if you turned all your lump sum into a guaranteed lifetime income. If you plan to spend a chunk of your retirement money don't include that sum in the amount you used to calculate your potential annuity income. You can't have your cake and eat it; and you can't have your view of the Taj Mahal at sunset and expect the money you spent on the airfare to be keeping you in chocolate digestives in 20 years' time.

Putting the sums together. If you add together the pension you can expect from your employer and the state, and the annuity your various assets will buy you, that will give you an idea of the income you will be able to expect. You'll now have a much better idea of the extent to which this measures up to the figure you blithely set down in answer to the question, 'How much will I need when I retire?'

What can I do to increase my retirement income?
If there's a gap between the income you want in retirement and the income you can expect – and the gap's not in your favour – you'll need to do some extra saving. To calculate how much that will need to be, refer to Table 8 below. It takes you through the steps (using the same annuity rates) of calculating the regular yearly saving you'll need to do from here to retirement *if* (and it's a big *if*) you can count on a regular 3.5 per cent return on your savings over and above the inflation

---

Table 8 **How to calculate how much you need to save** (assuming, rather implausibly, no change to life expectancy or interest rates between now and your retirement)

This table assumes that you can make a steady 3.5 per cent on your investments, over and above the rate of inflation. It starts out by reporting the price insurance companies are currently charging for an annuity to last from retirement to the day you die (or the longer lived member of a couple dies, where appropriate).

Note that the price of an annuity will rise as life expectancy rises. It will also be affected by interest rates: higher interest rates make it cheaper to buy an annuity; lower interest rates make an annuity dearer.

The table then sets out what it costs you to get £1,000 of annuity, in each category, with the same caveats.

And finally, it shows what, on these assumptions, you would need to save faithfully each year, and invest wisely in something earning a real 3.5 per cent in order to achieve a retirement annuity of £10,000. You can calculate your own savings target from that figure.

Annuity rate:
Amount you get for every £1 of purchase price:

Single man, retiring at 65	0.15
Single woman, retiring at 60	0.13
Couple, man retiring 65, woman 60	0.12

What it costs you to get £1,000 annuity is therefore:

Single man, retiring at 65	6,693
Single woman, retiring at 60	7,874
Couple, man retiring 65, woman 60	8,264

So for every £10,000 of retirement income, you will need a lump sum of:

Single man, retiring at 65	66,925
Single woman, retiring at 60	78,740
Couple, man retiring 65, woman 60	82,645

Therefore, if you have five years to retirement, you must save each year (assuming real returns, over and above inflation, of 3.5 per cent a year):

Single man, retiring at 65	12,481
Single woman, retiring at 60	14,685
Couple, man retiring 65, woman 60	15,413

. . . if you have ten years to retirement, you must save each year:

Single man, retiring at 65	5,705
Single woman, retiring at 60	6,712
Couple, man retiring 65, woman 60	7,045

. . . if you have 20 years to retirement, you must save each year:

Single man, retiring at 65	2,367
Single woman, retiring at 60	2,784
Couple, man retiring 65, woman 60	2,922

. . . if you have 30 years to retirement, you must save each year:

Single man, retiring at 65	1,296
Single woman, retiring at 60	1,525
Couple, man retiring 65, woman 60	1,601

. . . if you have 40 years to retirement, you must save each year:

Single man, retiring at 65	792
Single woman, retiring at 60	931
Couple, man retiring 65, woman 60	977

Note This calculation assumes the annuity continues to be paid to the survivor, in the case of a couple. Annuity rates are based on best available quotation. *Money Management* magazine, February 1989.

rate. That may only be possible for the portion of your saving you can do in a tax-advantaged way – through additional pension contributions or Personal Equity Plans.

As an example, if you've left it late, like me, to start a proper pension, and you want to add £20,000 a year in income to your company pension when you retire in, say, 20 years' time, Table 8 shows that (at present annuity rates) it will take regular savings of £5,844 a year from now till retirement to generate the amount you want. The bad news is that saving £5,844 a year out of post-tax income is a stiff task. If you pay tax at the 40 per cent rate, you would need to pour nearly £10,000 of your income each year into Personal Equity Plans (PEPs) for you and your wife to generate the retirement income you want.

Making use of any unexploited shelter in the tax rules on pension contributions will help to reduce that figure, because it will allow you to use pre-tax income (rather than post-tax income) to generate some of the savings. None the less, the challenge is a substantial one. If you (and I) had started saving even ten years before, the amount required each year would have been only £3,202, just about half as much each year.

More worryingly, perhaps, if you leave it till ten years before retirement to start building up that extra £20,000 of income when you retire, Table 8 shows that you will need to save £14,090 a year from now till retirement, the after-tax equivalent of £23,483 in salary to someone paying 40 per cent income tax. Not only is that a very large sum to save in its own right, the task is made much harder because its size starts to take it out of the range in which tax relief is available.

For example, it is far bigger than the maximum combined annual PEPs investment of a married couple – so if the couple's tax-sheltered pension fund contributions were up against the Inland Revenue limits, they would be left trying to achieve that 3.5 per cent return on at least a part of that sum while paying tax both on the income from which the savings must come and the dividends, interest or capital gains the savings generate.

The first basic rule of pension planning – you can't begin too soon – has a telling force when you start racing against the clock to build up a retirement income.

Figure 5 Sample calculation of saving for retirement

Retirement date : 2010 , 20 years to go

Current expenditures: £2000 a month, £24,000 a year

Net Adjustments after retirement :
(- work travel, kids, housing + holidays, golf, car)   — £3000 a year

So adjusted living expenses after retirement : £21,000
                    (in today's money)

Assuming current tax rates continue, that will require gross income
of roughly £28,000

Work pension = 25/60 ths

Current salary of likely retirement grade : £30,000 a year.
So pension will be : 25/60 x 30,000 = £12,500 in today's money.
Additional voluntary contributions will generate annuity of £10,000 in
money of 2010. Assuming 5% inflation rate between now and then,
using conversion factor of 0.38, that works out to £3,800 in
today's money.

No preserved pension

State pension : £2,266

No Serps because contracted out

First stab estimates of post-retirement income :
     £12,500
+   £3,800
+   £2,266
=   £18,566

Gap with required income : roughly £10,000

Profit on sale of house : £50,000 in today's money
(assuming house prices rise no faster than inflation)
Would generate an index-linked annuity of £5000 approx.

Remaining income gap : £5000

Required savings to generate that annuity : £50,000 in
today's money.
Savings required over next 20 years to generate that sum : £1,768 p.a.

And that's not all

Alas, there is more bad news to come. First, inflation doesn't stop when you retire. So though all our calculations up till now have been to provide a satisfactory income in the first year of your retirement, that extra £20,000 will get progressively nibbled away by inflation. If you lived for 20 years after retiring, and inflation averaged five per cent a year during that time, your income in your last year would buy you only £396 worth of goods, calculated in the money of the year you retired. At seven per cent inflation, the figure would be £277; at ten per cent, £164.

Not enough to live on. To protect yourself, you would have to make sure that you kept your capital sum intact each year in real terms, not merely in nominal ones – or you would need to buy yourself an annuity that promised an indexed-linked income, as some insurance companies now offer, or one that promised a guaranteed five per cent increase in pension payments. Either of these approaches would reduce the amount of annuity you would get for your up-front payment by about a third – meaning that to achieve the same desired retirement income, you would need to save at a rate roughly 50 per cent higher than outlined in Table 8.

You will also need to compensate for the fact that your company pension scheme is not obliged to increase pensions in line with inflation – though many try to make some increase, regular or occasional. That means having to save enough extra money to offset the shrinking purchasing power of your company pension.

And, of course, these calculations assume that you intend to consume all your capital, except perhaps for your house, by the time you die. If you hope to leave a substantial sum of money to your children or your favourite charity, you will need to save at a still faster rate, to be sure of having a lump sum as well as the amount needed for the annuity calculation.

How to keep saving for retirement when times are hard

■ The most difficult thing of all is to keep stashing away money for your future when it's all you can do to keep up with the present. There are no instant answers – but some combination of the following steps might help:

■ **Build saving into your budget.** Don't just save what's left over at the end of the year; set yourself a target for retirement saving that's as firm as any of your spending limits. Even if you have to lower the target a bit when the future looks gloomy, try to build a realistic budget that includes saving for old age as well as spending for the present

■ **Don't be too heroic.** It's tempting, when you've started on a long-term saving plan, to try to stick rigidly to it in every year. It's certainly desirable to save consistently, of course, but don't burn yourself out by trying to keep to a saving target that economic circumstances are rendering impossible. Better to bend than break: adjust the target downward – but keep saving *something*

■ **Earn as you save.** If circumstances prevent you from meeting your saving target out of your main income, consider doing a part-time job or some freelance work with the intention of putting the money you earn straight into savings (less a small 'extravagance tax' to reward yourself)

■ **Watch for bargains.** If the amount you're putting aside isn't as much as you'd like because the economy's in poor shape, make it work doubly hard by taking advantage of the potential bargains in under-priced shares, unit-trust units and other investments that are usually to be had when gloom prevails. That doesn't just mean buying something that's come down in price a long way; try to look for securities that represent assets worth more, in quantifiable terms, than the price the paper is selling for.

One of the few consolations for a gloomy day today is the hope of a better tomorrow. Keeping up your commitment to saving for the future is a practical way of reinforcing that hope.

Start now!
You will have seen that detailed pension planning is a long-drawn-out and – unless you have started early enough and stuck religiously to your yearly saving targets – frustrating business.

So the lesson of this chapter is that, if your preliminary calculations suggest you will need to top up your ultimate pension with some savings of your own, even if only to protect it against inflation, you will make life a lot simpler and more pleasant by starting as early as possible to put *something* aside.

That holds good even if the immediate outlook is gloomy; and the accompanying message is to keep on saving, even if at a reduced rate, during bad times as well as good.

CONCLUSION

Next Steps

If you've read through the preceding chapters, you'll have some idea of how to protect yourself and your family against a chilly economic climate.

The book will only be of real value, however, if you use it to build your own defence, in advance, against the threats that a poor economy poses at work and in your household finances. That's what this chapter aims to encourage you to prepare – a systematic plan, tailored to your individual needs, for putting the seven steps into action.

How to build your own action plan

Building an action plan involves looking back through the seven steps in this book and extracting the practical actions that are relevant to *you*. If you're not a boss, the cost-cutting expenses in Step 2 will only be relevant as part of a know-the-worst exercise, not as part of an action plan; if you're single or don't have children, part of Step 6 won't be relevant; and so on. But each reader is likely to find something relevant in every chapter; so write down the action points that matter to you.

The next task is to decide the priority of the actions. Don't pick and choose: plump for the chapter heading that most closely fits your immediate concerns, and focus on the actions from that chapter that you've singled out as relevant to you.

Now turn those actions into a timetable, with the survival stages following on from the assessment actions. You don't need to carry out the actions marked with an asterisk until you're convinced a recession is imminent; save those for a 'to-do-later' part of the timetable.

Once you've dealt with the action items in the chapter that's your top priority, select the next most urgent chapter and go through the same exercise. Do it again with your third priority chapter.

Three chapters' worth of actions are probably enough to be going on with; set the others aside until you've made headway with the first three chapters' worth.

At this stage, your action plan and timetable should look something like this:

JB-ACTIONS   April 1990

Priority chapters:
Step 1, job
step 4, finances
step 7, retirement

Priority actions:
Step 1:
A. Devise plan to reduce job dispensability (THIS MONTH)
   especially:
   i) Make data more relevant (BY SUMMER).
   ii) form internal alliances (START NOW)

B. Assess own dispensability (THIS MONTH)

C. follow up with actions if necessary (START NEXT MONTH)

D. Plan to create promotion opportunity (THIS MONTH)
   Target: ask for promotion in 3 months' time (DATE
                                    IN DIARY NOW)

Step 4:
A. Devise budget that will allow creation of annual
   surplus (NEXT MONTH)

B. 3-year plan to increase qualifications (BY AUTUMN)

C. Set up contingency plans for mild recession (THIS MONTH)

D. Investigate short-term borrowing power if crunch comes
   (THIS MONTH)

Step 7:
A. Calculate likely pension (BY SUMMER)

B. Compare advantages of Additional Voluntary Contributions,
   free standing AVCs and PEPs as home for surplus
   (BY AUTUMN)

C. Plan to put money in one of them by end of tax
   year (BY END MARCH)

At the end of each month try to tally up how far you're sticking to your timetable, and how successful your efforts have been. Try to build concrete objectives into the plan. If you're attempting to gain promotion or a pay-rise, allow yourself three months or so of preparation – 'adding value' to your job, giving yourself a higher profile, and so on – and then make an appointment to see your boss to make your request. Don't expect this, or any part of your campaign, to pay off magically by itself: you'll need to ask, politely but persistently, to achieve the pay-off.

Watching for the red light

Mark the actions you need to take right from the start. But you should be ready to put the rest into effect once you're convinced that a recession is imminent.

Warning signs you should watch for fall into two categories: those for the economy as a whole, which you'll have to keep an eye on in the newspapers; and those for your particular industry, where the best guidance will come from your own grapevine of informants (among your customers and in your own and rival firms).

Warning signs in the wider economy

1. **Unemployment numbers.** If these start to rise again, after a long period of decline, treat it as a warning signal. The important unemployment figure is the seasonally-adjusted one, excluding school-leavers (who cause temporary bulges in the labour force that don't reflect underlying economic trends).

   Also keep an eye on the seasonally-adjusted figure for the total number of people in work: once that starts to fall, it's another warning sign. In both these cases, one month doesn't mean much, nor probably do two in a row. But once you've got to three, it's a good sign that the early stages of a recession are under way.

2. **Monetary policy.** The thing to watch out for here is evidence that the Government is tightening monetary policy, even though the economy is already starting to slow. This is a good warning that the Treasury is sufficiently worried about inflation that it's prepared to run the risk of a recession to see it brought down. So if the Bank of England puts up interest rates, even though there have been a few months of reports of a slowing economy, storm clouds are hovering. The key figure is the banks' base rate, which is directly influenced by the Bank of England. When that moves, you can be sure the Government is putting on the squeeze.

3. **Rising bankruptcy figures.** These are not a particularly good guide to whether a recession is *coming* , since it takes companies a while to get into enough of a mess to call in the receiver. They are, however, a good guide as to whether you're actually in a recession, and they're often available before the official economic estimates come out.

4. **Downward trend in the CBI survey.** Every month, the Confederation of British Industry takes the temperature of its members, asking them how confident they feel and how expansionary their plans are. The 'confidence' number usually gets the headline attention, but it's not always very reliable – businesspeople's confidence is a bit fickle, and it can be overly pessimistic.

   More interesting are some of the subsidiary questions, about whether member firms expect to hire more staff, and how big their backlog of orders is. Watch out for sharp downturns in these numbers. The CBI index requires a bit of familiarity to interpret, so the best guide is probably not the raw numbers themselves but the commentary offered by the newspapers' economic correspondents. And, as with all these other indicators, a downturn in the CBI index alone doesn't tell you a great deal – you have to take it into account as one possible indicator along with all the others.

5. **A consistent downward trend in important economic sectors,** such as retail sales and construction. Demand for houses is particularly sensitive to interest rates, so it's been particularly battered recently. But the construction industry as a whole is still working off a backlog of orders in commercial

property, and is looking forward to some government road-building contracts. So the traditional indicator – housing starts – probably isn't very reliable as a guide to the overall health of the industry.

This is one of those cases where straightforward observation is as helpful as elaborate statistics. Keep an eye on the skyline: are there more cranes, or fewer? If you know anyone in the building trade, how easy is it for them to find new work or new contracts? What's happening to applications for planning permission? And so on.

Similarly, observation and anecdote is as good a guide to retail spending as official figures. Ask your friends if they're spending money; watch for the timing of sales in shops, and how long they last; keep an eye on activity in the local high street. In all these cases, the advantage of observation is that it's *local* : it tells you what the economic climate is in your region. If your firm sells nationwide or internationally, of course, that's not such a helpful guide. But if the firm has a particular concentration of sales close at hand, which is often the case, the state of the local economy is all the more important.

6. **Classified job advertising.** Again, this is something you can watch both locally and nationally. If the national papers start to run noticeably slimmer job sections, that's a good early warning that recession – or at least an economic slowdown – is on the way. (Thursday and Sunday are the two most popular days for general job advertising, by the way.) Also, if you know anyone in the local job centre, ask how tight or slack the job market is. Similarly, find out from local temping agencies how good demand is compared with this time last year. (Temping is very seasonal, so direct comparisons of this month with last month don't tell you much; but the industry as a whole provides a sensitive barometer of how seriously companies are tightening their belts.)

As well as the economy-wide warning signs that everyone will be watching for, from the people you meet in the pub to the City economic analyst interviewed on the television, there are warning signs that bear particularly on your own industry.

Warning signs in your own industry

1. **Ominous noises from your big customers.** Listen to what your customers say about the state of their own businesses, and – allowing for the usual hard-luck stories – pay attention when it sounds as if things are turning down. Pay even more attention if your colleagues in sales find it increasingly hard to make a price-rise stick; get pushed into more generous discounting; or find the size of the average order shrinking.

2. **A falling-away of new prospects.** Find out from the sales and marketing people what's happening at the front end of the sales pipeline: the acquisition of *potential* new customers. This is a more sensitive indicator of bad times ahead than actual sales volumes or even pressure on prices, because those both happen at the end of the sales pipeline, and therefore lag a few months behind.

   If people are not responding to your promotional attempts – not filling in response coupons in newspapers or trade magazines, not calling up with sales enquiries, straying out of your sales outlets – that's a sign that the sales pipeline is emptying. In a few weeks' or months' time (depending on your sales cycle) you'll find those missing customers hitting your revenues, and hence your profits.

3. **Belt-tightening announcements from head office.** Like hard-luck stories from salespeople, you have to take these with a pinch of salt. These days, belt-tightening is a regular feature of corporate life, even in industries weaned on the expense account, like advertising and broadcasting. None the less, if your company's attempt to save on petty cash – cutting down on the number of magazines purchased and squeezing down on business travel – is matched by similar moves at rival firms, that's a good sign that the industry as a whole sees trouble ahead.

4. **Easier hiring conditions.** If it suddenly gets easier to fill a vacant job, that's a good indication that the economy's slowing. If it's a local, unskilled or semi-skilled job, that tells you more about the local economy than about your industry.

If it's a specialist job for which you'd expect applicants to come from a wider area, the information's a guide to activity in your industry. Remember to allow for seasonal factors and for the effort you put into recruitment this time as compared with last. But if, after allowing for that, there's still a markedly greater availability of potentially short-listable candidates, treat it as a warning sign.

5. **Sell-through and market research.** If you're part of an industry with a long distribution chain, remember to keep an eye on 'sell-through' – what happens to the products after they leave you and enter the rest of the distribution channel. You may be shipping away healthily, and so may your first-tier distributors – but if unsold products (yours or your rivals') are piling up on retailers' or wholesalers' shelves, that's very bad news.

    This ought to be too obvious a point to mention, but during every recession some big, well-managed firm with the latest computerized stock-management system takes a bath because it neglects to keep an eye on sell-through – so don't let it happen to you.

    Similarly, keep an eye on any industry market-research numbers that track intentions to buy your product, or monitor actual end-user purchases. Someone in your company or trade association will be collecting numbers like these. Make a point of bumping into them in the canteen or calling them up for a chat. That way, even if you're not on the official circulation list for these figures, you'll still get to hear how they're going.

Once warned, it's time to act

When you're convinced, from watching these indicators and listening to the pundits, that a recession is imminent, it's time to put the rest of your action plan priorities into effect. At this stage, you might want to take the following steps:

- Re-double your efforts to protect your job.
- Start to carry out your plans to help your company survive.

- Overhaul your household budget contingency plans.
- Consider putting the first belt-tightening measures into effect.
- Make sure you can pay any big expenses on the horizon.
- Check your options if you have to find a new job.
- Reassess the impact of a recession on your household assets.
- Check how your pension-building and family-protection plans will be affected.
- Set up an 'opportunity alert' for ways to take advantage of the bad times.

Taking these steps in advance will leave you much better prepared to cope with the onset of a recession; and preparation is half of the game.

The bare minimum

I can't leave you without suggesting a few basic things to do even if you aren't convinced that difficult economic times are round the corner. You can do them all in the bath tomorrow evening (as long as it's a good long soak) and still have time to listen to *A Book at Bedime* on the radio.

Five things you should do TOMORROW – even if you don't think there's a recession coming

1. **Work.** Assess how dispensable your job is – and how vulnerable you are in it. Even if you don't think the industry's about to be hit by a wave of redundancies, you can still do great things for your earning power, promotability and all-round happiness at work by following some of the advice in Step 1.

2. **Your career.** Think hard about what you want to be doing, what you're good at and how far your current job reflects it. If

you decide you don't like what you see, start to change it – using the long-distance fantasy planning of Step 5 as well as the more practical, short-term actions of Step 3.

3. **Your finances.** Even if you can't face calculating the full household-finances worksheet, try to work out whether you're putting anything into savings at the end of the year. If you're not, re-read Step 4, and see how you can trim back your expenses (or raise your earnings) to allow you to build a cushion for yourself and your family.

4. **Education.** Assess the investment in human capital you and your family are making, and start to think seriously about the economic impact of the educational decisions you're making for your children (or allowing them to make for themselves).

5. **Retirement.** Ask yourself just what provisions you've made for old age, apart from the state and company pensions. And, no matter how far away retirement is, resolve to spend an evening working through the mechanics of building yourself a satisfactory pension. Even if you have to guess at half the numbers necessary to do the calculations in Step 7, the exercise will still give you an overall feel for whether you need to be stepping up your saving, or whether you can afford to take it easy.

Last thoughts

The scale of the economic forces that affect our lives sometimes seem so vast that there's little we can do about them. Indeed, it *is* to protect yourself completely against inflation; and with all the career planning in the world, you still run *some* risk of losing your job in a recession.

But preparation, forethought and a certain sort of 'imaginative prudence' are the next best things to getting an advance peep at next year's stock prices.

This book, alas, cannot offer you the 1991 stock prices – or even the 1991 economic statistics. But it can offer you practical ways of building barriers around your life, and your family, to keep the bad times out.

The next recession, when it comes, may not be a bad one; the inflationary tide may recede again as quickly as it arose in the late 1980s. But no one who takes the advice in this book will suffer if the bad times turn out to be not too bad after all. And if the outlook does become as gloomy as some of the forecasts were suggesting in early 1990, you'll be glad you started building the protective barriers when you did.